Bl...

and

Priceless

crocus

C

crocus

Black and Priceless

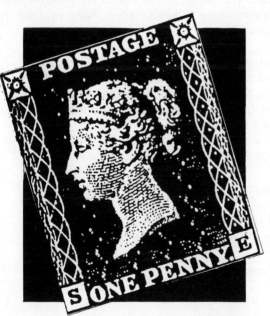

the power of Black ink

First published in 1988 by Crocus.

Crocus books are published by Commonword Ltd,
Cheetwood House, 21 Newton Street, Manchester M1 1FZ.

Commonword gratefully acknowledges financial
assistance from the Association of Greater Manchester
Authorities, North West Arts Association, Manchester
City Council, Calouste Gulbenkian and the
Commission for Racial Equality.

Typeset and Printed by Rap Ltd, Rochdale, OL12 7AF

British Library Cataloguing in Publication Data

Black and priceless; the power of black ink,
   1. Poetry in English, 1945 — Anthologies
   821'94'08

ISBN 0 946745 45 5

ACKNOWLEDGEMENTS

Whara Poseur. Arden College Image Magazine.

Hypocrite. Poetic Licence. 1987.

Tank Yuhn Breddah Garvey Moss Side Write Autumn 1987

Untitled. England No Mudder Country. Apartheid.

First, Second/Third winner respectively Cultureword Competition 1987. Poetry Section.

Woman. Black Rose. Moss Side Write Magazine Autumn 1987.

Skin Skin Yuh Know Meh Highly Commended 1987 Peterloo Competition Afro-Caribbean/Asian Secion.

Lure of Cascadura. Winning Poem. Peterloo Competition 1987. Afro- Caribbean/Asian Section. Published The Guardian April 24th 1987 and Poetry Matters Autumn 1987.

New Spehres. New Horizons. 'Nia Zindagi. Nya Jevan'. The Kennebec. The Adventures of Maud Mellington. First, Second and Third winners repectively of the Cultureword competition Prose Section 1987.

ACKNOWLEDGEMENTS

CONTENTS

Young Writers

PREFACE
by Benjamin Zephaniah

Black and Priceless is part of an uprising, an uprising of the voice of a people whose voice has been suppressed. Do not take these words lightly, they are about *now,* they are about a people who live today, they are *live and direct.* These words come from a generation who have no real voice in the society. They are their own historians; the historians of the future shall have to relate to them if they are to obtain an insight into Black British life in the 1980's, an insight which is more truthful than, and an alternative to the soap operas we see today, which we are told 'represent us'.

What must be noticed is the scope and range of this uprising, this generation needs its Ranters and Protesters to keep its roots and question itself. But artistic writing and the art of writing does not need to suffer because people are angry, and *Black and Priceless* proves that. The styles differ as much as the personalities creating the writing. There are many shades of Black, and the fact that we are writing our own history makes this priceless.

Benjamin Zephaniah is first and foremost a performance poet, a writer and a musician. His most recent publication is **'The Dread Affair'** published by Arrow Books.

FOREWORD
by Kanta Walker

A writer does not write in isolation for herself or himself, but wishes to be read. It is the first step towards recognition to be seen in print. Black writers have had to cope with greater barriers to have their work published and then it has been marginalised. I am very proud, therefore, to be given the opportunity to read some excellent work in this anthology.

It is difficult to point to one piece of work and talk about its excellence when all the contributors are of such high quality. I have enjoyed reading Patrick Elly's poems for their rhythm and language. John Lyons's poetry vibrates with energy and points to the bitter truth of the reality of living with racism. *Englan No Mudder Country* - sums up our Black experience but we have come of age now and the anthology is a tribute to that. Naya Aghebo and Anne-Marie Thompson both write with a clarity and thrust that is refreshing. Cindy Artiste has style, and I hope she will continue to see her work in a dramatic context. In *The Red Death of Edgar Allan Poe* Lemn Sissay invokes many powerful spirits.

There is not enough space to write about all the individual contributors but they are all 'a good bunch'.

I found reading Peter Kalu's *The Adventures*

of Maud Mellington , hilarious and very witty. It is an excellent story in the right setting and rich in local colour.

Qaisra Shahraz, Deeppa Banerjee and Debjani Chatterjee's work fills a gap — there are few Black women of Asian origin writing about cross cultural experiences.

I wish them all a bright future.

Kanta Walker is a visual artist and writer. She is presently working on her second novel after the success of **Sare Mare** *published by Pandora Press.*

INTRODUCTION

For centuries Black people have excelled in the art of conveying their thoughts, feelings, experience and culture through poetry, story telling, plays, carvings, hieroglyphics, paintings, songs, music, dance and many other 'recognised' art forms. These modes of expression have survived to this day despite being misunderstood and misrepresented, for one reason or another. Black literature was therefore ignored and viewed as sub-standard supposedly because in many ways it diverged from the European norm of writing.

This collection uses one medium — the written word; from a diversity of Black writers in the community. For one person writing may serve to be a statement, for another the flow of words are written to satisfy a creative urge.

It is not unusual therefore that much of the work within this publication deals with racism in one form or another. We cannot offer guidelines on how to read the work — but to ask you to try and 'read' the thoughts between the lines and to see the ways in which racism affects our lives and in many cases forces us to justify our existence within this society.

The stamps used in this anthology illustrate the family origins of each writer and are thus the symbolic signposts charting the spread of the diaspora through the four corners of the earth. The priceless Penny Black symbolises that time in history responsible for the dispersion of the global Black nations; we have proven ourselves a determined people struggling through to win our rightful place in the 'First World'.

Cultureword through Commonword aims to promote, encourage and support Black writers towards print and then expand into other areas such as performance and any other innovative ways of expanding the creativity of the writer.

Gratitude must also be expressed to Rushiraj Munshi (Film Maker and script writer), Valerie Bloom (writer and performance poet), Fiona Walker (artists), Fitz Lewis (Identity Writers Workshop member), for taking on the arduous task of selecting work for the book.

To Judy Craven (Afro-Caribbean Language Unit), Kanta Walker (writer & visual artist), Benjamin Zephaniah (writer, performance poet and musician) for their professionalism and members of Commonword's Publications Committee for their support and guidance.

Special thanks go to Lemn Sissay, not only as the first person to hold the post of Afro-Caribbean/Asian Development worker for Cultureword; but also for organising the first Cultureword poetry and prose competition in 1986, from which a major part of this work was selected.

CINDY ARTISTE

I am Black American who has been resident in Britain since 1979. A professional playwright my recent productions have included Face Value *(Contact Theatre Company 1985).* Half Hearts and Quarter Measures *(Avon Touring Theatre Company 1987) and* Dreams with Teeth *(Contact Theatre Company 1987). I am currently adapting Alice Walker's* Meridan *for the stage.*

NEGRITA

I could hardly believe it —
Me!
Being called 'Negrita'
and pursued through medieval Toledo
by a skipping school girl
tendering a yellow flower.

Me!
who was more or less
minding my own business
on the banks of the sudsy Tagus
when a swarm of apprentice Catholics,
becoming possessed at the sight of me,
made me, IT, flapping their uniforms
in my wake.
On a dare. One
follows too close behind
treading on my cheap sandals
snapping a thong and my mood
of patient astonishment,
I turn, they yelp
and scatter, re-flocking
on the sunnier side of the street.

And suddenly I am beamed into this advert:
you know the kind of thing —
cute kid/plenty of sunshine/yellow flower —
and I am being called 'Negrita'

and offered a weed
by way of apology for breaking my sandal.
And it's so corny I want to laugh and
toss the flower-child into the river.
It's so corny I want to tell her
'Look kid, I'm from the First World
so keep your diminuitives to yourself.'

I take the flower.
Yeah me.

When out of nowhere swoops
some bony old bird
in last year's mourning
who shakes the child, clucking abuse
which I can't begin to deflect
with my O-level Spanish.
And it's so sad that ...
It's so sad that I —
Ah, shit,
I chuck the flower,
breaking it carefully beforehand.

DEEP

The ruby is missing
and the emerald
and the know-how to survive their excavation
by other tongues
with other x-marked maps.

But pennies
tossed behind my back
and copper-bright wishes
fall home
here
in the well of beginning.

I leap and am lost,

A flutter of tongues —
an untutored try
at sonic communication —
the vibrations dun
my ears only
confusing my balance
and I am stranded,
my treacherous tongue
changing allegiance midstream
and luring me deeper.

To save myself
must be my first concern.

Then to talk
write
rant of such depths.

To save myself
I rise
purposely slowly
warned by the pressure in my ears.
Behind my eyelids I see now
the death masks
of the dead drowning.

They smile.

but still I rise
summoned
by a red sheen
denoting sunlight.
I wash upon a hot dry bed
all seeming-silent
till I place my ear
to your navel
and hear — again!

The Sea.

Dr DEEPA BANERJEE

Born in Calcutta in 1953, I spent my childhood in various countries and in boarding schools in India. I qualified as a paediatrician and worked for a charitable clinic in Delhi. At present I am a housewife and mother of two children.

BECAUSE

Why should I write a poem?
So many have been written.
All the ones that ages wrote
assail my mind unbidden.

Words are suspended, meant for reading,
for reflecting —
and for cradling every soul.
Shades of comfort, tears of sorrow,
gently linger —
aging to oblivion's goal.

If I offer less than this
I offer bitter passion,
smoth'ring in a cloud of hate
some guilty self admission.

Dr DEBJANI CHATTERJEE

Born in Delhi in 1952, I have pursued an education in Japan, Bangladesh, Hong Kong, Egypt and England. I work as a Community Relations Officer. I have been writing since childhood and won the Shankar's International Children's Prize for poetry in my teens. My poetry and articles have been published in magazines and anthologies in Britain and India.

POEM IN THE POST

A glance at the bought postcard
and glib phrases reappear:
'having a wonderful time ...
sun 'n' sand ... wish you were here ...
love ...'
No, I will not send to you
postcards for acquaintances
to be treated to envied
suntanned holiday instances.
Love,
I shall send you a vision
of our future together,
I shall post you a poem:
crystallised perfume of rare
love.

TURMOIL

They had anonymous faces
distorted in bemusement.
The crowd roamed at random
like crazed and headless chickens
rushing around the cracked pillars
that hold up an uneasy canopy
of brewing doom and storm.
They had jagged edges
frayed by the blare of loudspeakers.
They had tattered smiles and scattered
                                    twitches.
They had lost their equilibrium.
Even watching them seemed to embroil
and contaminate one in their constant turmoil.
They shouted meaningless obscenities.
They breached their inner peace
like caged neurotic birds that pick at
                                    themselves.
They were a disturbance, a seething mass
of poison frothing over a bubbling stew.
Their business was affray.
Like riotous puppets testing the length of
                                    string,
they danced their epilectic dance
to the hackneyed tune of the manipulators
it was election time again ...

YOUR STORY SITA.

Dutiful daughter, perfect wife,
devoted mother, best of women,
role model for all time —
Sita, you are all these things.
Fragile and gracious, you are the unknown
                                    quantity
lending confusion to the well-known epic,
the pivot about which both heroes and villians
                                    turn,
you look on all with fortitude,
lady of sorrow, magnanimous,
woman of power, race ancestor.
From childhood I have unravelled your story
within the glorious annals of the race of
                                    Raghu,
a lone figure of heart rendering dignity,
a love match on which heaven showered petals
                                    and blessings,
a legendary loyalty that survives each
                                    incarnation.
Against all advice you stood by your man:
you entered the wilderness and turned your
                                    back
on steamy jungles of fratricide, corruption and
                                    greed
where men jockey for power in barbarous
                                    rituals.
The first version heard is the sanitized one

where the brave prince wins you after
                              remarkable feats.
But your quiet presence fills those spaces
where questions reside. How was it from your
                              point of view?
After so many adventures, battles won, demons
                              subdued,
lovers united, triumphal return of king and
                              queen,
an exemplary life full of noble ideals ...
suddenly one realises the ominous meaning
of the fire test that you came through
unscathed — or did you? —
specially devised for women-goddesses,
a testimony to man's fickleness and impurity
that makes him suspect it in others,
a test that needs performance for evermore.
From the blaze when you lifted scorching eyes
to the crowd with shuffling feet and bowed
                              heads,
did you foresee the dowry-deaths your
                              daughters yet endure?
The base filth of gossip could reach royal ears,
to pull down paragons from their pedestals.
Banished from the bosom of your loving lord,
your other half, you became a single mother.
In my childhood I vainly searched
for the 'happily ever after' denied you
— and denied me. But this was an honest
                              lesson.
You story, Sita, is more than fairy tale.

REFLECTION

Grandparents sit with children,
still, for once, on their knees
all smiling, all smart,
in the sunshine garden.
Captured for posperity
is all the family togetherness,
the sense that we go on forever.
My shy cousin leaning her plaited head
on the grand wicker armchair
is married now to a business tycoon.
The spoilt little one looks up
from kohl fringed eyes
and shows off his fire engine painted red
and unique in the neighbourhood
for its strident sound.
My sensible brother stands on the edge
but still manages to give the impression
that he is shepherding us children in.
My sister's expression of concentration
is the same one I often see
on my nephew doing homework,
there's a faint look of anxious-to-get-away
and I remember all the adventures
of that garden just beyond the picture frame:
the crocodile and bank game we played,
especially hilarious in monsoon weather
the temple worship for which we gathered
flowers, leaves and stones,

taking it in turn to be head priest,
and how carefully we observed the rule
about removing our sandles and canvas shoes;
we played at patriots too and drove out the
                                                              British
again and again ...
My grandfather is sitting ramrod straight,
the head of the house, a self-made man
with a title from the Raj for services
rendered a war-time Ministry of Defence.
His patrician nose on a stern brown face
belies the warm and gentle eyes.
My grandmother sports the largest red dot
on her forehead and her round face
beams her pleasure, her gusto in life.
A red bordered white sari drapes her head,
a handsome woman, full of strength.
I am standing self-conscious
and holding up the lacy new frock
so that the knickers peep at the camera.
Somewhere in the middle of the picture
I am posing and doing my duty.

PATRICK ELLY

*Give thanks and praises to the Most High for
the inspiration to write these poems which
are* livicated *to all good people.*

HYPOCRITE

Aey hypocrite
Mi know yu plan
Mi know yu seh yu gat a wicked intention
So nuh badda try fi come
Wuk yu brain pan I man
Yu check seh yu smart
But yu was a fool from de staat
Caw yu neva carry
Nuh love inna yu heart
Look how yu mek
De people de a suffah
Look how yu mek
De yout dem a cry
All becaw yu cyaan satisfy
Caw every word outa yu mout a lie.

Back weh!!
Wah mi seh?
Once bitten, twice shy
So nuh badda try
Fi come wuk yu brain pan I
Mi sus yu out good an properly,
An, mi know yu plan
Mi know seh yu gat
A wicked intention
But it mus go wrang
Eh bound fi go wrang
So gwaan man

Galang
One ah dese days wen yu tink seh
Ah peace an safety
Yu know a wah?
Sudden
Destruction
Sudden
Destruction
Sudden
Destruction!!

TANK YU BREDDAH GARVEY

Tank yu breddah Garvey
Tank yu sah
Tank yu fi tell I bout Africa.
If I neva see yu.
I nu know wah I wudda duh.
Far yu was de first one
To tell I n I bout I homelan
An ever since dat day
I became a new man
A real man
A African.
How dignified and proud I am
To be a member of de race
Dat first gave dis world civilisation
Tank yu breddah Garvey
Tank yu sah
Tank yu fi tell I bout Africa

KARRYN EWERS

I am of Black British West Indian Cultural heritage. My mother is Caucasian (British Born) and father originates from St Elizabeth, Jamaica.

I am 24 years of age, Rastafarian in my beliefs, and I live as such. I have been writing poetry for the past five years.

Since attending a cultural heritage event two years ago, Africa and apartheid, have become the main subjects which I base my writing on.

JAMAICA   55¢

APARTHEID

The promised land as quoted.
Will flow with milk and honey.
But as we have come to know
Actions only speak with money.
So they've crushed the hands of Black men,
They've claimed our Fathers' land,
Took over all our people
Turned our rich soil into sand.
Destruction has appeared
To death our people go,
And violence war and crime,
Is what they've come to know.
The shooting of the guns
Cries: echo out this hell,
They only wanted equal rights
But who were they? Who could they tell?
Which led to brethren killing brethren
Becoming children of the night.
Then mourning all their sorrow
Which made them harder in their fight.
Remember; The iron fists of Black man
And the breaking of the chains.
Are supposed to mean our freedom
But aparthied still remains.
So what's happened to the system?
Still aparthied's going on.
If we stand — unite together
Soon aparthied will be gone!

SUA
HUAB

*I am 19 years old, and have been writing
poetry since I was 15. I am Somali/Black
British, born in Wigan. At the moment I am
attending Leeds University doing a degree in
Social Policy and Sociology — but still
writing.*

ONCE UPON A TIME

I cut myself really deeply once
But the wound would not bleed,
I tried to let it heal alone
But I needed help,
I thought the world would notice,
But no-one ever did,
I thought that it was obvious,
But I must have imagined it,
Ever so slowly the pain subsided,
But never quite completely,
Gradually and painfully
I felt as if I was beginning
To recover,
Then one day it beld,
Relief and numb shattering pain
Filled me,
To be replaced later
BY calmness and hurting,
At last I knew where I hurt,
And why,
I admitted I needed people,
And they came,
I felt better,
Not its gone, the scar has healed,
But, inside me,
Deep inside,
Sometimes in bad weather,
It hurts,
How it hurts.

LET ME

Let me do what I would choose,
Let me love and hate without limits,
Let me be myself for a change,
Let me care if I want to,
Let me be alone if I ask,
Let me say what I think,
But please let me write,
Let me..?

PETER KALU

Born 1962, Manchester. Mother: Danish, father: Nigerian. Lived the life of an intellectual till 19 — exams, exams, exams — then discovered sex and other pleasures. Fell in with a number of dangerous thinkers and emerged as a member of the Peoples Writing Group. *(since named the* **Identity Workshop***). Married with two sparkling daughters. Now studying Law at Leeds University thanks to the* **Marcus Garvey Scholarship Award 1987.**

The Adventures of Maud Mellington.

Number 1 : Dirty Laundry.

Finally, incontrovertibly, she was going to do it.

As Maud made her way to the newsagents she thought about the course her life had taken. It was a strange thing, life. There were always ups and downs, good times and bad, and it all happens so quickly. She had been lucky to meet the right man so early in her life. A lot of people she knew had gone through chops and changes with their men, but not her. When they had first met in Jamaica back in '48 at Martha's leaving party, they dove-tailed instantly. How he was handsome! Those big pearl white teeth that he flashed to show off the gold filling at the side, and his slow chicken leg dance. He really had won her heart with that dance.

She was 22 at that time, and had quite a few admirers around her. Yet she and Maurice stayed together. Life was wonderful — full of warm nights, tears and laughter. He called her his 'passion fruit', his 'living jewel'. She called him 'peach knees' and 'ocean lips'. Around about then, he qualified as a joiner and left Jamaica for a short stay in England to make his money, or so he had planned. Several long letters and two years later she had joined him in England. Even then, with both of them together, the good job and money didn't arrive. But the children did. First Delroy, then Julie a year later, Jerome a year and a half after that and then Mark five years after. Each one had been a different birth.

Those days, when the children had been just babies, had been the most chaotic of all. Their father worked long hours as a road sweeper - coloureds did not get skilled manual worker jobs, he had been told. He would come home tired, so tired, and never did the two ends meet. She had nursed the babies, cooked and clean-ed, washed and sewn, and they had seen each other through.

One day, September 15th 1966, quite suddenly, he collapsed at work. He lay there with the sweepings, his big bristle broom still clutched in his hand, Eddie, his workmate had said. They lifted him up and carried him to the road sweeper van then laid him out in the back and drove him to the hospital. He died an hour after arrival, before anyone had managed to contact her and his last words had been, 'Tell my wife not to worry, I'm going home.'

Maud crossed the street and headed for the junction with the main road.

The family had been in dire straits then, with no

pension money or insurance coming in. She had got a job as a machinist in a garment factory which she held down for 16 years until she was laid off during an economy drive. As she was getting slower with her hands then, she knew that she was unlikely to be taken back on. Delroy, after a few incidents, had settled down into a mechanic job and was doing okay. Julie was flying high in London as a personal secretary to a window frame company director; Jerome had left home some five years back and run off with some girl she had never met — good luck to them, and Mark was at college, though he would never say what he was studying. They had all left home. Of course they would visit her now and again, and Delroy and his wife would bring their children. She had three grandchildren, Joshua, Nathan and Afrika. She enjoyed babysitting.

The past eight years had gone by with friends she had made through the years who she would go out on the town with every other weekend on a soul shakedown, though she only danced the slow songs much to the delight of the men who liked to take it further (and occasionally she let them!), with the T.V. to fill some lonely hours and when the children and grandchildren popped in, and with books. She had always wanted to read books. She had taught herself the meaning of most of the long words she came across, like 'incontrovertibly', with the aid of a large dictionary. She enjoyed reading. Detective stories were her favourite: the bookshelves of her front room were packed with the detective adventures of a host of astute criminologists. In fact, after a year or two reading crime fiction, Mrs Mellington began to realize that, through it, she had developed a very sharp mind: she had acquired many of the qualities of the protagonists in the novels — attention to detail, logical analysis of the situation, a good, though not yet totally, photographic memory, and an almost intuitive ability to identify clues. She had frequently surprised herself by being able to predict accurately who would be the guilty party or parties at first two and three, then five and even six chapters before the end of a book, even the ones with the most convoluted plots and bizarre, erratic characters.

Maud turned left onto the main road. The newsagents was only two blocks down.

It was the need to do something useful again, to live her own life independently rather than have it revolve around that of her children that had first prompted Maud to think about finding something new to do. She had scoured the local paper chasing worthwhile jobs but to no avail. She had racked her brains to come up with something that she would enjoy doing and be good at, and that would take her out of her house. Now she had found that something. Certainly, she had done enough preparation for it, what with eight years of related research. And if people raised their brows at her for choosing such an occupation, well let them hurl the stones.

Mrs Mellington pushed open the frosted-glass, burglar-alarmed newsagent's door. The bell above it made its usual metallic clatter. It was undoubtedly rusty. She closed the door behind her, shutting out the din of traffic. The shop had the smell of stale bread and newsprint about it. Sunlight was pouring in through the large display window lighting up the vast array of packaged sweets and chocolates beneath the plastic screen by the counter. The shopkeeper shuffled forward from the back quarters where he had probably been settling over a cup of cocoa, watching the racing. His name was Mr Jones. His first name was Chancery, but she called him Mr Jones, seeing as she hardly knew him.

'And what can I do for you today?' said Mr Jones in his practised, attentive manner.
   'Come to place a card in the window', replied Mrs Mellington, then plucked the item out of her bag.
   'It's 10p a week', informed Mr Jones, 'how long do you want it in?'
   Not having his spectacles, Mr Jones held the

card at arm's length and attempted to read it.

'Keep it in a week. Should be long enough, thank you', replied Mrs Mellington.

Mr Jones, never in a rush, squinted at the card, and read it aloud:

'Pensioner ... turns ... Private ... Investigator ... Competitive ... Rates ... Phone ... Mossway 433.' As the meaning of the words sank in, the shopkeeper looked up slowly. 'You are a Private Eye?' he asked, incredulously.

'And why not?'. Mrs Mellington smiled. 'I'll pay you right now if you don't mind.'

'Certainly.' The shopkeeper paused again, curious. 'I'd never have guessed,' he confessed, 'I'll put it in the window right away'.

He did so and so her plan was well and truly in place. Mrs Mellington returned home satisfied.

That same day at 3pm, in the back kitchen of a house in the same area, Cornelius Hayes, sole tenant, was bent over a cubby hole by the sink looking thoughtfully at two black plastic bin liners, each bulging with dirty laundry. Cornelius had a dry, soiled shirt in his hand. He folded then crammed the shirt into the liner designated for dry. That bag was three quarters full of dry, the other one quarter full of wet clothes. Laundry had been on his mind all morning. He knew it was soon time to carry out the next check on the launderette. It all would have been so much simpler if the sun had been out for the last three weeks as he had expected when he had confidently hand-washed the clothes that were now in the wet bag. But, as if in conspiracy with the other event, the sun had stayed away so the back yard washing line was useless. It would take three days to dry one line of washing without the sun and the chances were, most of it would 'disappear' in that time. Cornelius Hayes was fast running out of wearable clothes, and worse still, he knew the dirty laundry was starting to fester and smell badly — the stink had reached even into the upstairs bedroom.

Of course the Pastor had called round after the funeral and offered him help. He had been too shocked at that time to think of anything he might need doing. And when the same man called round again when he had not turned up at church on account of not having had any decent clothes, he had not let the Pastor in because of the smell. He told him through the letterbox that he would be coming back into the church in a month, but needed some time alone, to himself; he told the same story to his domino friends when they called round. By then he hoped to have got rid of the smell.

Cornelius was not afraid of the launderette. After all, he owned a five function LCD quartz watch and could change the battery in it. So he was not dazzled by a lot of buttons and technology. It was the people he was uneasy about. A man ought to be able to wash his clothes in private, not in the full glare of whoever walked in. And so it was that he determined to find out when no-one was at the launderette, if there was such a time. He would go then.

Each day, with notebook and pen to hand, he went to visit the launderette and noted down the time he got there and how many people were inside. He had done a whole week and it seem-ed that Tuesday morning was clear. But he wanted to be sure. So he was going to do one more week to make sure there was a pattern. He was due to set off for an afternoon check.

The launderette was only three shops down from the newsagent. It was as he was about to step into the newsagents that he noticed the card in the window. It startled him: 'Pensioner turns Private Investigator. Competitive rates'. Quickly, he withdrew his notebook and pen from his car coat pocket, and jotted down the Private In-vestigator's 'phone number.

This was the ensuing telephone dialogue:

'Hello, could I have Mrs Mellington, Private In-vestigator please.'

'This is I on the line an' speaking to you personally.'

'I got some work for you, perhaps. How much you charge for the day?'

'Various rates depending on the work involv-ed. (Pause) From five to twenty pounds plus expenses.'

'I'll take the five pound rate please, it's an easy thing.'

'Before I can settle with you on the rate, exactly what is the nature of the work?'

'It's a highly confidential affair.'

'I don't deal with marital disputes.'

'No, I mean I can't talk on the 'phone about it.'

'Very well, we can arrange to meet.'

'Must be some place quiet an' private.'

'Yes, I understand. You living aound Mossway?'

'Happens I am at the moment.'

'Do you know Alvino's cafe?'

'Yes. The one corner of Whitby Road.'

'That's it. We can meet there. It's a quiet place, no one uses it,and quite out of the way.'

'At what time?'

'I'm very busy at the moment but I can fit you in at 10.30 in the morning tomorrow.'

'That's good.'

'I shall be wearing a purple, veiled hat and a brown three- quarter length coat. Arrive there at 10.30 sharp and I shall be waiting inside for you. We can talk then.'

'Three-quarter length?'

'Yes. Three-quarter length.'

'Very good.'

'I charge £5 for the interview.'

'Alright.'

'See you there then.'

'Yes.'

'Goodbye for now. Pleased to be of service.'

When Maud entered Alvinos at 10.25 am that day, she met a gleaming new decor and a pursed-lipped, smiling proprietor at the service counter. Maud approached him and ordered a coffee. Al obliged. She then walked back to a corner table by the door, sat down, took off her veiled hat and her gloves, and sampled the coffee. It was strong, possibly Brazilian blend and piping hot. Mrs Mellington was nervous about the looming rendezvous. The fact was just beginning to register in her mind that she could potentially be running a serious risk. Had she been foolish? Suppose she was asked to shadow an assassin? Or infiltrate a drugs ring? Or even just drive a car? She did not yet know how to drive. Working on solutions, she decided she could call a taxi; jumping assassins were out of her skill range, and drug ring infiltration was a matter for the police not her. Anyway, the man on the 'phone did not sound like the KGB or the CIA or the MI5. In fact, he had a local accent and had hesitated when she had mentioned her fee. His voice had been mellow. She guessed he was in his ripe sixties. With thoughts such as these Mrs Mellington calmed and composed her mind.

Cornelius Hayes arrived at Alvino's wearing his last set of clean clothes: — pin-stiped trousers which had last seen daylight twenty-five years ago at his daughter's wedding and leaving party — they left for Canada straight after the party;

the starched white shirt with the detachable collar which a youth at church had described as wildly old-fashioned; a woollen V neck jumper he had worn on the voyage to England, and kept ever since and the C & A coat that the wife had bought for him only two months ago for his birthday. He had wanted to treasure the coat in memory of her, but here he was wearing it out. Feeling slightly starchy on account of the shirt and collar, and sandpaper dry due to having taken a bath early in the morning prior to the appointment, Cornelius slowly pushed open the cafe door. His eyes wandered up and down. There were a few men playing cards up front, a woman, veiled hat by her side, to the far corner. He approached the table of this woman.

'Mrs Mellington, private investigator?' he whispered.

'That's right. And you are Mr Hayes?'

'Yes. Cornelius Hayes. Pleased to meet you'.

Cornelius sat down. The manager, focusing on the new arrival, approached the table, waiter style, and prepared to make a sale. He smiled his smile. Maud smiled back, waiting for Mr Hayes to take his cue and order something. Cornelius wondered what all the smiling was about and whether the two knew each other. He also noticed the fresh paint on the walls. The waiter enquired as to whether the gentleman wanted to order. Cornelius bought a coffee for himself and offered to buy Mrs Mellington one too. She accepted the offer.

'Shall we discuss work?' proposed Mrs Mellington once the coffees had arrived.

Mr Hayes leaned back on his chair and looked at Maud. 'I want you to do a stake-out', he announced solemnly.

'Stake out what?' was Mrs Mellington's reply.

Mr Hayes did not waste time. 'A launderette'.

'A launderette', echoed Maud enthusiastically, greatly relieved at the sound of something familiar.

'Yes', confirmed Mr Hayes.

It was then that he had doubts. The lady did not look like any private investigator he had seen before. There again, no two private investigators looked alike. But this woman looked like a housewife through and through. He had expected a more shadowy shady type. He quizzed her: 'You have done this type of work before?'

Mrs Mellington's professionalism was being questioned. She rose to the demands of the occasion: 'certainly', she replied, 'stake ins, stake outs, stake 'em all abouts, medium rare, rare medium or plain as you like! You name it, I've done them all,' she rapped with aplomb.

Mr Hayes could not help but smile. Maud pressed home her advantage:

'Your enquiry regards the surveillance type of stake of course. Now which launderette do you want staking out, and where is it?' In her mind, Mrs Mellington had formulated her first, golden rule of detective work: when in doubt, bluff.

'The one on the main road,' said Mr Hayes, 'the information I require is, when is that launderette not being used by anybody and yet still open to the public. And how much it would cost me to wash two bags of clothes there.'

'I deduce you want to use the launderette when no-one else is there?'

'That is correct. I have done some staking out of the place myself. The details are in this book here, you may find it useful'.

Corneilius passed his notebook to Mrs Mellington. Maud accepted it, then swallowed some lukewarm coffee and considered the facts. Following classic lines of analysis, the man had obviously got something onto his clothes, or the clothes of one of his accomplices, that he wanted to remove. Ignorance was bliss and would probably prove profitable, but she could not get implicated in crime. She needed to know.

'Tell me, Mr Hayes, why do you not want to wash the clothes when people are around,' Maud asked, 'you haven't been in a robbery or something?'

Cornelius laughed at the cheek of the woman. He relaxed and confessed frankly, surprising even himself with his candour, 'No it is the embarrassment to wash your clothes in public, and I is a old man. Is a woman's job, nuh?' he said.

'The good lord gave us each two hands,'

countered Maud.

'Will you do the job or no?' asked Mr Hayes suddenly impatient, 'give me a straight answer.'

'Yes, I'll do it' said Maud, 'it means sitting in the launderette all day, every day for a week until I find for sure when no-one is using it. And doing that for two weeks to identify the pattern of the customers. That will cost you plenty.'

'How much?' asked Cornelius cautiously.

'At £2 an hour for nine hours a day for two weeks, that's going to be £200 pounds at least.'

Cornelius groaned. He had never considered that Private Eyes might be expensive. He had a little money still, in a Post Office account, but he was saving that for his funeral.

He looked so handsome when he was sad. She was attracted by that oceanic, far-away look in his deep brown, steady eyes and wanted to do him a favour, maybe get to know him. 'I have a better idea,' she said, 'I've a friend who takes in laundry. What if I find out if she can take in yours and how much it would cost you. How about that ?'

'That sounds good,' Cornelius replied, his eyes sparkling like cresting waves.

Maud drank a mouthful of the now tepid coffee. Mr Hayes gulped some of his own.

'So, I will report back to you tomorow morning with the information. My fee for the work will be £5. Is that good? '

Cornelius smiled, content. 'Good'.

'Write your address down here in case I need to contact you,' Maud concluded. She passed her own notepad across the table to Cornelius. 'Shall we meet here again at the same time tommorow and I can tell you what I find out?'

'Yes, that will be fine,' said Cornelius, who couldn't help admiring the woman's easy efficiency, wit and poise, though her dress sense was eccentric.

'O.K. Same time, 10.30 sharp,' she said. Mrs Mellington put on her hat then looked around. 'Now, I shall leave first. Please leave three minutes after me, Mr Cornelius. I shall treat everything said as confidential between you and me. I hope you do the same.'

Cornelius gave an affirmative nod. Mrs Mellington put on her gloves, eased her chair back then got up and walked calmly out of the cafe. Mr Hayes ordered another coffee. He left three minutes later.

That afternoon Belinda, trade-name Mrs Lather, was hard at work in her humid cellar laundry. Laundry was Belinda's livelihood, and the eight by six by five feet cellar was her living quarters for six hours of every day. It was a sanitary looking, functional place. The brick walls had been plastered by her son and painted matt white, the ceiling was also matt-white and adorned with a lattice of co-axial power cables that ran doggedly from socket to meter to extension to socket, sometimes held in place by brass clips, sometimes held by tape. Hairline cracks radiated from the heavy-duty, strip lighting.

The layout of the laundry machinery was ergonomically sound: to the right, in the corner furthest from the door, two mammoth white-enamelled washers, with small, squat double glazed and steel rimmed doors churned round and round; these were umbilically connected to a sinkplace by their rubber effluence pipes, which chugged and gurgled through washes and spins; nearer the door, still to the right the driers whirled, their large round windows revealing waltzing, blue tagged sheets; a stack of folded white laundry bags lay beneath the driers and a high speed extractor was nested under the meters by the far wall to the left - both meters and extractor regularly whirled at considerable speed; parallel with and close to the left wall were three lines of open topped laundry bags, each bag representing a job lot and bristling with the same colour code tags; the bags were arrang- ed by method of priority — the line nearest the machines comprised those bags which were to be processed first, the bag nearest to the washing machines being the first in the line; a rack steel-bolted into the nearside wall served as a spare pair of hands for folding sheets; all ironing took place upstairs due to the limits of space.

Among the mounds and machines moved

Belinda. That day at 2pm she was clearing the No. 2 washer. The sleek black pistons of her forearms slid into the machine and dragged out a sodden mass of washed sheets, then steered them into the plastic basket waiting below. She swivelled round with the loaded basket, hands wedged in the handle slots, raised her back upwards out of its 90 degree angle, braced, then manoeuvred the basket two feet across to the extractor. The extractor stood 4ft tall. It was top-loading. At 5ft 4in Belinda found hoisting baskets up to that height troublesome. So she was in the habit of depositing the basket at the extractor's base and loading it piecemeal. It took three stoops and scoops to empty a basket. As she commenced the task, the door bell jangled, its jangle cutting through the dull cacophony of shuddering machines.

Belinda lead Maud through the house and down the cellar steps, then went on with her work.

'Fine afternoon today,' said Mrs Mellington.

'You're not due for your wash yet are you?' said Mrs Lather by way of reply. It was unusual for Mrs Mellington to drop by on a Wednesday.

'No, I've come to talk to you about some work,' answered Maud.

'Well you go right ahead and talk, don't mind me,' said Belinda as she lowered the extractor hood and leaned on it. 'How are the children and the little ones?'

'Fine, fine. And your son?'

'Same as he always is.'

'The business going well?'

Belinda pointed to the lines of laundry. ' Busy. Yes, very busy.'

Belinda paused, thinking. Washer 1 would stop in ten minutes, the sheets in drier 1 would be dry; washer 2 needed to be reloaded — the last wash cycle of the day, drier 1 could take the load currently in the extractor, so could drier 2 in another 20 to 25 minutes. Drier 1's sheets would need to be folded; then everything in the post-drier bags to be taken upstairs, ironed and despatched. The ironing could start once the washers had finished for the day.

Looking around, Maud noticed the tags on the clothes, and the slight leak at the base of the number 1 washer door which had already eaten through the enamel and was rusting the metal. The washer door needed a new rubber seal. She was sweating with the humidity and uncomfortably conscious of the washing powder chemicals hanging in the air. She unbuttoned her coat and, feeling slightly dizzy, looked for something to sit on. Belinda noticed Maud's discomfort and pointed to the sink unit.

'Lean on that,' she said sympathetically.

'It's a mystery how you manage to keep going, to me Belinda. A mystery.'

'I've been telling myself that for the past five years, but you get used to the heat 'n' fumes,' said Belinda, advancing towards drier 1.

Maud remembered what she had come for. 'Now how can I start? I met a man, a fine man.'

Belinda stopped. 'Don't you always?' she joked above the clatter, gurgle, slosh and whirl, 'just pass him over to me.'

'He asked me to find out if you've got room for his laundry.'

'That depends, will I be doing his things regularly?'

Maud had not asked Cornelius that. She decided for him. 'Yes. But he's down to no clothes now, except what he's wearing - things he's dug out of the 'back-back' of his wardrobe that smell like cheese and rotten egg and look crumpled like a crisp bag. So I told him I'd see if I can fix him up with you.'

'When does he want it done for?'

'As soon as possible. Like I said he's got nothing left to wear.'

'I'll take him on, since it's you that's doing the asking. But I'm very busy right now.' Belinda pointed to the bags full of unwashed laundry. 'Can he not use the public laundry, if it's so urgent?' she asked.

'The man is vain', Maud said, 'he doesn't want anybody looking at his clothes'.

Mrs Lather smiled. She pulled the last sheet from drier No 1. Then turned round to face Maud. 'Alright. I'll put him in as soon as I get him. What's his address?'

Mrs Mellington ripped a sheet out of her notebook and passed it to Belinda.

'You came prepared,' said Belinda accepting the sheet and glancing at the address on it.

'Part of my new job, this equipment,' beamed Maud, patting the notebook then returning it to her coat pocket.

'And what might that be?' enquired Belinda, intrigued, as she handed Maud a folded laundry bag and a set of purple tags.

'I'll tell you tomorrow when I collect my laundry', replied Mrs Mellington, giving nothing away.

'I see,' nodded Mrs Lather who knew she would find out in the end, if not from Maud then from one of her other customers, 'now you tell this man of yours to tag all the clothes and things and stick them in that bag. My son will collect them tommorow and every other Wednesday — which means he'll call Wednesday at 6pm and the bag will be returned Thursday or Friday at the same time.'

'What's the cost to him?' inquired Mrs Mellington, remembering the details.

'For the one bag, same as usual — £3.50 from dirty, to clean - pressed, collected and delivered. '

'Good', said Maud. She wrote that down. Then she put on her hat then picked up the bag and tags again. 'I'll be leaving now, you've been a great help'.

Belinda was waiting for more than those words

of thanks. She had worked out that Maud had probably become a traffic warden. 'Go on then, tell me', Belinda coaxed.

'Oh the new job?', said Maud, savouring the moment. 'I've become a Private Investigator — a Private Eye.' With that Mrs Mellington headed quickly for the cellar steps.

Mrs Lather shouted up the stairs at Maud's back: 'Now don't you come down here telling me them type of stories and expecting me to believe them. Private Investigator! You couldn't investigate a blocked sink!' She returned to her laundry and wondered if it was really true.

The next morning — Wednesday 10.30, Alvino's cafe was visited by Maud Mellington and Cornelius Hayes. Ostensibly drinking morning coffee, they in fact went over the details of the agreement negotiated with the launderer. Cornelius was satisfied that it was a good deal — the day and time were not inconvenient and the price was reasonable. He declared that he was looking forward to some fresh clothes and paid Mrs Mellington her fee, shook her hand, hugged and thanked her.

Wednesday at 6pm the laundry was collected with no hiccups.

Thursday afternoon Mr Hayes received his fresh clothes.

That same evening Mr Hayes went to the local library and with the aid of a telephone directory did some detective work of his own.

Maud answered a knock on her door on Friday morning to be handed a spray of Interflora flowers and a thankyou card, together with an invitation to an evening meal — all compliments Cornelius Hayes. Mrs Mellington went back indoors and considered her position. She decided that, done properly, her new job would hold few dangers and many pleasures. She decided to take it up full-time.

All characters are fictional and any resemblance to any persons is entirely by coincidence.

LIFE FORMS

Burnished bronze
Kisses the hay-mud.
Shags flap
As songs
Of buttered breeze
And brushing reeds
Cry out
Jerk-taste
And slurp
The earth juice
In this field
Of glistening
life forms.

AFRICAN ARK

It sailed
In the Beginning
With stout faith mast
Thru turbulent
Thru perilous seas
And yet was not
Overwhelmed.
Festooned with
Strength and heart.
Well able to set
Its own course:
After the forty days flood
Clear of old rocks
Lusty toilers
Tacked hard
Towards the
Green lands of
'We'll start again
without the engulfing troubles'.
Culture ship,
Never capsized.
African ark.
It sailed.
It sails.
And in its wake
Ever expanding waves
Of peace kiss only
One world shores.

DODOS AND AFRIKAANERS

Dodo. Didus ineptus
Pigeon drop ... drop ... drop ... drop ... dropping.
Flap waddle
Flap waddle, flap waddle
Swish-waddle. Waddle-waddle.
Waddle ...
Dinosaur didums:
Dodo didn't
adi ade adu ada adapt.

Dutch journey-on seaway settler.
Tried to be an Afri-
Can't
Tried to be an Afri-
Can't
Tried to be an Afri-
Can't:
The Afrikaaner can't
adi ade adu ada adapt.

FITZ
LEWIS

*I was born in Clarendon, Jamaica raised by
my grandparents; my grandfather had a strict
attitude to children and their education.
Despite being able to read the Bible and
daily newspapers at pre-school age, I did not
reach great academic heights. I emigrated to
England in 1960 and had to shelve any
ambition to become a writer due to the
pressure of employment. I started to write
anew in 1985, giving up full-time work a year
later.*

TODAY'S YOUTH

Parents toiled decades away
Hope now abandoned on scrap heaps
Their descendants
A lost generation
                dole trapped
Eyes spell disillusion

Like talented seedlings
in the desert
They wither away
No jobs
        what hope is there ...

Life's basic needs
for them
Far out of reach
Their world immobile.

Ambitions crushed
Their future ...

JOHN LYONS

*I was born in Port-of-Spain Trinidad moving
to Tobago aged 9 on the death of my mother.
I arrived in England in 1959 to study at
Goldsmiths College, School of Art London;
then to Newcastle-Upon-Tyne University.
Throughout my teaching/lecturing career I
have also been active as a visual artist. I have
exhibited extensively throughout England and
also in Holland and Paris.*

*My love for writing has remained constant
and bears a reciprocal influence on my
painting. In 1987 I won the Peterloo Poets
Afro-Caribbean/ Asian prize, and received a
"highly commended" for another entry of
my work in the same competition, and a
"highly commended" in the Poetry Society
National Poetry Competition. In the 1988
Peterloo Poets Afro-Caribbean/Asian
Competition I won joint second prize and a
commended prize for a second entry.
Publications include The Guardian, Poetry
Matters Autumn 1987, the Poetry Society
National Poetry Competition Prize winners
anthology and New British Poetry 1968-88.*

SKIN SKIN YUH KNOW MEH

Soucouyant, Soucouyant,
ball of fire vampiring through the night,
I found your skin beneath a water barrel
 and salted it,
 and salted it:
 'Skin skin, is me, yuh na know mi,
 skin, skin, yuh na know mi'.

No more banquets of blood,
no more purple rings
on my skin in the mornings;
no more chalk marks: crosses and noughts
on doors and windows to keep you away;
I found your skin beneath a water barrel
 and salted it,
 and salted it;

In daylight, you, an old woman leaning on a
           stick,
shunned the chalk line across your path;
you raved and cursed
marking your next victim with blaze of your
           eyes.

Children taunted you.
 'Soucouyant, Soucouyant!'
But I found your skin beneath a water barrel
 and salted it,
 and salted it,

'Skin skin, is me, yuh na know mi,
skin, skin, yuh na know mi'.

LURE OF THE CASCADURA

Exiled under silver birch and conifers
I see the poui and immortelles blooming;

the mistle-thrush sings,
    but I hear the kiskadee
    'Qu'est ce qu'il dit,
    qu'est ce qu'il dit.'

Blue crab scuttle in mangrove mud
where the forest floor is a compost
of dead leaves;

that grey squirrel is no agouti
sniffing the air for hunters in rain forest;

I listen to the birch's sigh
and hear distant rain approaching;

pewah and pomme-arac
usurp the taste of peach and Cox's pippin;

but I have savoured the cascadura
spiced with legend and must return to die
where the scarlet ibis flame.

THE BLACK POET

Black,
without camouflage
where the car-
nivorous 'pandas' run.

We are the hunted
by un-natural selection.
We learn to fashion
weapons of wit in poetry:

No subtle
diplomatic metaphors,
or hypocritical similies,
but the hard, sharp antonyms
of confrontation
expressed in black and white.

JAB JAB

Out of masquerading crowds
they came shuffle-dancing:
jingle jingle, jab jab,
jingle jingle, jab jab,

jester-clowns
in brilliant satin,
armoured against the lashing whip;
stuffed up like bobolee,
black face in white face wire mask;

we are di boys, jab jab,
from Fyzabad, jab jab,
we fraid nobody, jab jab,
we big and bad, jab jab,
we lookin fuh trouble, jab jab,
in Port-of-Spain, jab jab,
an ready an able, jab jab,
jingle jingle, jab jab,
jingle jingle, jab jab,

arms circle in air,
whips flash, crack like gunshots,

before we go away, jab jab,
yuh goin to pay, jab jab,
cause we ded trouble, jab jab,
an big an able, jab jab,

pennies fall like rain
ringin on tarmac:
they fill purses,
shuffle-dance away,
jingle jingle, jab jab,
jingle jingle, jab jab,
jingle jingle, jab jab.

SUNSEEDS OF SLAVES

The new sunseeds of slaves
sprouting up through rubble
in England's cityscapes.

In this city bush
no navel strings are buried;

no sufferings eased
by sighing bamboo grove.

Lost are the earth's wisdoms
passed through digging fingers
familar with yams and tania
in Carib soil.

Across the generation gap
words like stones are pelted
against the living brow-bone:

but theirs is a more urgent pain.

ENGLAN NO MUDDERCOUNTRY

Englan no muddercountry.
Ol West Indian 'istry book
was tellin lies:
is white man mamaguy.

Englan
no 'Land of Hope and Glory',
ask de so-called black minority,
dey go tell yuh a different story.

Buh Englan
'Mother of the Free'
yeh, free to burn a Pak,
free to mug a Black,
is a fack:

Man, dis is National Front country
wid aerosol can graffiti:
'Gas the Blacks',
say di writin on di wall.

Here any Black man can carry
di collective identity:
wog, nigger, alien disgrace,
slum-maker, wife stealer,
contaminator of di English race,
job-tief, sociological case;

an yuh tellin mi
Englan is muddercountry,
Cheups !!

JENNY MacDONALD

Born in Jamaica, I have lived in England for the past 25 years. I am 49 years of age and the mother of two 'boys' aged 26 and 19 years. I am a State Registered nurse by profession working in a school. I have been writing for the past five years, mainly short stories.

WOMAN

I hold my head up high because I am
Proud to be called a woman.
I want the thought, the respect and
the love I deserve, as a woman.
I don't want to run, to hide, to cry,
To suffer rape and disregard.
A second class person because,
I am woman.

I want my spirit free deservedly.
Because I am woman.
I want the time to spend every day.
Thankfully that I am woman.
I refuse to be caged and suppressed,
oppressed,
Left to rot, in time forgot.
Because I am woman.

I want to love and be loved in return.
To feel warmth and tenderness.
I want to bear children and hear
them call me mother.
And in my fading years when my
eyes are growing dim
I want to look back, and with a prayer upon
my lips.

Be happy to say,
Thank God, I was born Woman.

DONNA MONTAGUE

My parents emigrated here from Jamaica in the early '60's. After a brief residence in London, they moved to Sheffield, where I was born and brought up. I am currently pursuing a degree in American studies and writing at Crewe & Alsager College. I hope to become a journalist after graduation next year.

JAMAICA $1.50

THE KENNEBEC

'Jeb, there's someone out here wants some gas.'

'Be with you in a minute. Why don't you serve them?'

'It's Wily Jake, he asked for you by name.'

'Okay. I'm coming.'

I left what I was doing and, wiping the oil off my hands onto my overalls, I went outside to pump the gas. Wily was out there alright, resting his huge arms on the open truck window. Soon as he saw me he started clearing his throat knowingly though he never spoke a word. I didn't ask why he wanted to see me, just filled his tank and asked for twelve dollars. Looking me right in the eye he peeled the necessary greenbacks from a wad he'd taken out his shirt pocket. I took the money though his thick fingers seemed to grasp it tightly for an instant before he released it into my hand. Then he drove away, tight-lipped, his face very red. I went back to the garage....

I'd heard there was a great turnout at the funeral but I wasn't able to go since my parents strictly forbade me to. I can understand the way they feel. If anyone was to be blamed ... Later the people started shaking their heads and a few of the heartless ones asked without shame, their words dripping inference, how such a tragedy could have happened in such a small town. I remember well everything that happened that day but I still can't figure out why I lost her. All they understand here is fishing and potato growing. How can they comprehend the real extent of the accident? She had died. But in a way so had I. I'd loved her too much, and I'm not going to be corny or anything, but her death was totally in vain. If anything good was going to come from the whole polluted affair I should have to live, and suffer, and then perhaps in time she would forgive me, quit holding the soul in me, release me to die in peace. She might even be waiting for me....

It all happened about two months ago on that stretch of the Kennebec which is near Interstate 16. There the soil is useless and a lot of thick wiry grass grows. That August was the hottest in my whole life so you can understand why I was feeling kind of logy that day.

'Hey, slouch anymore you'll be mistaken for a jelly fish.'

'Sorry. There are no jelly fish here, Susan.'

'No? Well there will be in a minute. Why are you smiling like that Jeb? You're not about to die are you, or be converted by the 'gentle yet sweet sting of Our Lord's antiseptic?'

'Maybe I am.'

'What?'

'I said...'

'Are you okay?'

'A moment ago you said I looked...'

'Sure, sure. Listen, can you stop it? Just stop

whatever it is you are doing that's scaring me? Something about you today is really giving me the willies, brrr.'

'I'm sorry.'

'Will you stop apologising?'

'Okay.'

'Good. Come to the movies with me.'

'Nah. I'd rather sit here and listen.'

'Hand me the hammer Jeb.'

I was holding it, staring at a face both foreign and familiar that was mine in the bright metal.

'Oh, for Chrissake here.' I lobbed it. Karl caught it with a gloved hand and grinned. Yes, she had a sharp tongue alright. You could say she was a little pushy, a little mannish. She'd not let it go at that. She persisted.

'Listen to what for Chrissakes?.'

'The water. It's hard to explain ... you remember that time we went to Virginia and we stood on the hill overlooking that gigantic field?'

'Wasn't that something..? Are you trying to tell me you've come face to face with your own mortality and you're no longer afraid?'

'No.'

'Then why don't you shut up. Jeb I'm going for a dip. Join me?'

I shook my head really slowly because I had a headache. I picked up a small rock and saw a funny little orange bug clinging to it. Then I tossed it into the river. When I looked up I saw Susan frowning. She went a little way up the river and began to strip off.

It was a rare thing for Wiscaset to have such a fine day. As I narrowed my eyes to the spangled flickering of sunlight on water I thought surely this was a day for flinging open cupboards and doors and cellars and hearts and minds. A day for airing secrets and clothes.

How right I was. If only I'd told her from the beginning how I felt, what I wanted.

(But though he felt that way there was something dark as a raincloud moving and shifting within him. He could hear her gasping and splashing in the water but he did not look up. Instead he plucked a blade of grass and wrapped it around a finger. The grass here was dry and yellowing. When the breeze blew it made a ticking sound).

'Jeb, I need some help over here.'

'Yeah, I'm coming. I'm just…'

'Jesus what's the matter with you, are you blind or something?'

'I didn't see the stupid toolbox.'

'You'd better go and get cleaned up. Put a plaster on that, you know the junk we handle round here.'

'Jeb?'

She must have made her mind up some time ago but had been too scared to tell me. When she called to me like that and I turned round she was trembling and I don't think it was because the water was cold. I don't think so.

(When she called him she startled him. He inhaled sharply. Susan. How long had she been there? He could not turn round right away because the bad thoughts were now jumping and twitching in his head like sunbeams so he had to wait for them to settle back down into darkness. When this happened and he turned a kind of smile had fixed itself onto his face).

She started twisting a few strands of her long blonde hair around her finger. Her head looked sort of shrunken with her hair wet like that. She looked about thirteen years old instead of eighteen. It took a while before she looked him in the eyes. I guess I knew what was coming the way a bunch of dark clouds signify rain.

(Slowly their eyes met. Her's jerked away then settled again upon his which were blue and open as the cloudless sky except for the tiny black pupils.)

'Jeb I'm ... I think maybe we should cool off for a while.'

'Okay, where?'

'I don't. I mean, I think we shouldn't see each other anymore.'

'Sure Susie, I understand.'

God I said that. I really said that to her, and I was smiling too I remember. But I know it wasn't a healthy smile. More like a grimace. Susan, she sort of stumbled taking a couple of steps backward. I don't know what it was she saw in me then. Maybe I looked a little crazy, just a little offkey. I must have been trying to avoid an argument. My head was much too tender to take one.

When she saw the smile twitching on his face it made her uneasy. She took a few cautionary steps backwards thinking 'Good dog, good Jeb,' remembering the time Mr Bonner's rotweiler had advanced, snarling at her.

'You're tired of me and my happiness makes you especially bored today.'

'That's a pretty wild statement. Just what are you saying.'

'I only know if you know what it is you're saying.'

'You know damn well what.'

'Yes I guess I do.'

'Oh come on Jeb, I only meant…'

'What you couldn't say. Softening the blow, I think they call it.'

'If that is the way you're going to be about this…'

When she sounded off like that I just crumbled. She was trying to make me feel guilty for something that was all hers. I knew just what I wanted from her that day though I never put it consciously into words. I was feeling something of the rarity of the fine weather. I wanted to make the day memorable. I wanted us to cosumate our relationship, but she didn't understand and it just cracked me up. She started getting all flustered and biting her lip and clenching her fists like petals.

'Okay, okay I'll make you understand! Remember what happened that time we doubled dated with Stephen and Mary and I had Stephen for the evening?'

'He was hurting you.'

'No Jeb. You see that is where you are wrong; where you always go wrong! We were just fooling around you know, but you always get too close. Too Goddamned close. Even here. I can feel it even here.'

'So you don't want to see me anymore, Okay. Fine.'

'God! Stop smiling that way. You were never so mean to me before.'

'I always assumed you knew what was best for yourself. You do know don't you?'

Suddenly he was not smiling anymore. It was as if something had cast a shadow over his face make the feature wary. He waited for her to answer him. He wanted her to give the right answer.

I know how completely uncalled for my question was. Of course she knew what was best. I didn't deserve her. I remember how she sort of held her breath looking down into the river. Then she sighed and when she looked at me again I saw tears in her eyes, but she didn't cry like most girls would have. She looked really serious for a moment. And tired. I wasn't making it easy for her. I was tempted to apologize but my head was hurting so much and I guess I wanted her to suffer. I think I wanted her to feel the way I knew I must be feeling deep down under the confusion: very hurt. But then she toughened up. Told me I was bugged, that I should get out of the sun before it set on me. Stuff like that. I wanted her more than ever by then.

The summer was ending and we would be going away to college. I'd be in Portland and she would be in Bangor and the way things were going that day it looked as if I was going to lose her entirely. As it turned out I did. Because then Stephen came. I know I'd been wrong about him. He proved to be the best man in the end only then I had this terrific grudge against him and I just couldn't shake it off. And he was always talking to Susan. We hung out at the river a lot that summer before the accident. If only Stephen hadn't chosen that day to come.

We'd been by the river maybe forty minutes when he arrived. He came down the embankment laughing and waving his shirt. He couldn't see me at first because I was half laying down in the long grass. Susan was putting on the rest of her clothes. I could tell she was angry by the way she kept flicking her hair over her shoulders.

When he saw Stephen something snapped in him. His last chance was gone. He played all his aces badly. She had come with him to the Kennebec. She had swam naked in the river before him, yet he failed to respond appropriately to her. He failed to make her want to respond to him. Instead he had sat and dreamed a silly dream about taking her away north to Moosehead Lake and conquering her beneath the stars before returning home triumphant, totally at her command and she at his...

I saw his lips moving but I couldn't make out what he was saying. Just what he said it didn't matter then and I'll never know now anyway. Stephen was wise, he left home about a month ago. We could never stay in this town together. Not ever. When he spoke to Susan she sort of sniffed and looked up at him. He put his hand on her arm and she moved closer to him and put her arm round his waist. She bowed her head and her hair fell forward over her face. I knew she was angry and upset. I also knew that she was finished with me but I just couldn't accept that. Not then. Not there by the Kennebec on the hottest day ever when my head was bursting with questions and questions and I wanted her but couldn't tell her how or why. I decided on one more shot. I had to have one more chance. If I killed her I never meant to, you see I was desperately in love. I could never do that.

I went after Stephen. I yelled to him to leave her alone and he said something like, Oh, it's Jebby, and laughed. I ran and grabbed him, then we were fighting and Susan was shouting and sobbing. She kept saying leave him alone, but I'm not so sure who she was talking to. Probably him, you see Stephen got quite a battering but I lost the fight because Susan ran up the hillside and disappeared over the rise.

I only found out later what had happened from my parents because her mother had phoned them. They've never spoken to each other since. The Kennebec is about a quarter of a mile from Interstate 16 and she hadn't for some reason used the subway.

'Jeb?'

'Why did she have to die Karl? I loved her.'

'I know. Look Mr Bonner's outside. He wants some gas and he's asking for you. I don't know what's going on round here. People are crazy. Tell you what, I'll say you're too busy right now. It'll be okay.'

'Thank you Karl. I don't think I can....' Things are so cold these days. The Kennebec is probably frozen over.

All characters are fictonal and any similarity to any persons is entirely coincidental.

MONIKA MONTSHO

I am a Black working class lesbian born in Middleton, Manchester, and now living in Moss Side. I train six days a week at Tae Kwondo, weight lifting and powerlifting. I have always been a writer in one way or another and am sure that I shall write as long as I live. My poetry is a reflection of my life and experience.

UNTITLED

I thought I could be one of the crowd
I learnt for a while to be coarse and loud
Emulating those I considered my peers
The weirdos, the dope heads, the dykes and the
queers.
But even then I lived in an Utopian world
Because in first and in last I was just a Black
girl.

I tried to change, to adapt in some way
It almost worked I felt, until one day
A racist came up to me and smashed me in the
head
And left me on the street, I might have been
dead
But they don't care, they doing you a favour
Getting rid of blacks is tough unpaid labour.

NAYABA AGHEBO

Born in Leeds I studied History, Education and English at Manchester University where I gained my B.A.

I have been writing poetry and prose since primary school. It is not my intention to offend nor is it to compromise my opinions as a Black woman in order to fit in with that which is perceived as the 'norm'. Instead I hope to strike a chord of unity with the proud and priceless, Black readers of this book.

NIGERIA

AUSTRA-LIAR

You aborigine:—
200 Years
Celebration
  of what?
    Raping.
      Stealing
        Pillaging
Seems to be the nature of the beast.

They took your land.
Stole your crops,
Took the women,
Stole your names,
Killed your animals,
Abused your culture.
Seems to be the nature of the beast.

Sent from Europe
  Criminals.
    No hopers.
    Trash.
Sent to pollute your green and pleasant land.

Proudly now they celebrate
  their
    200 years.

More years than blades of grass

Have you been there
Yet a stolen 200 years ... makes them feel

good.

Seems to be the nature of the beast.

JUST A THOUGHT

Every great man
Is of woman born.

Respect my womanhood.

TRINITY

The trinity
Holy father, son, spirit ...?
No.
Today is
Mother, child, giro.

When she was young
She was told
Her pen would soon dry
That a hockey stick, bat, ball
Would fit her hand better

No don't read those books
They'll just confuse your mind
Just remember netball tomorrow.

So, she left at 16
Couldn't get work
Tried.
What's the use?
Met a cool guy.
Said he'd take care of her.
But all he did was hustle.
Heavy under sensi
Left her chantelle.

So now the triangle is complete.

Unmarried mother, first child of many,
                              fortnightly relief
Maybe one day
Frying green banana
Or bent over dirty nappies
She'll check out that other trinity.
Pick up that book
Meanwhile she still prays to the bloody social.

SALLY NEASER

I was born in East Finchley, North London, October 1964. My mother is a Cockney from Mile End and my Father is Antiguan. I have only known my father for the last two years, so till that meeting I had no knowledge of anywhere in the West Indies, which was expected of me because of my skin colour.

I have no problems in expressing my joy on the birth of my son Jobe, March 1987. It is through my writing that I express the world about me, distant and on my doorstep.

THE BLACK ROSE

She fights up through the earth
Stretching her roots firm and long.
She stands out against the crowd
Silently, but strong.

Like a Goddess she stands perfect
As the sunrays shine and glow,
Upon her shape and glorious colour
Enhancing her dark features so.

Her graceful movement in the breeze
Like a swan gliding across the lake.
Swaying, as if dancing in beautiful rhythm
Bending, but she will never break.

Her petals reach out to the sun.
In her stem her life she sows.
There is no other so pure and powerful
As the flower we call the Black Rose.

FOR JOBE

You are me.
In you I see.
In you I feel love, hate, joy and pain.
I see your smile.
I feel your tears.
Your temper is mine.
I am your foundation for the future.
All that is mine is for you.
My pride is a precious thing.
Your father tried to crush it,
He denied you,
That cut deep in me.
Your cries for him pierce
but he will not be here with us
for I cannot take the wounds he gave.
Forgive me for that
I am your mother
but I am a person too.

PAULINE OMOBOYE

I was born in Manchester of West Indian parentage in 1958. I am a full time mother with four lovely, beautiful children, who are a great inspiration to many of my poems.

As a teenager writing poetry was an enjoyable pastime. It was much later in life that I realised that my writing was a positive form of communication. Not only enabling me to share my views, but giving me a tremendous amount of satisfaction.

Attending the Black Womens Writing Course (Cultureword) gave me the stimulus and encouragement to continue writing.

I have performed my poetry in various venues in Greater Manchester, Sheffield and Liverpool. I am now a member of Manchester's first Black womens' writing and performance group.

My work has been published in Moss Side Write, We Are Here, and most recently in *Sistahs.*

JAMAICA   20¢

I AM WHAT I AM

I am a Blackwoman
I am what I am.
I don't need no pity —
I don't need no man.

Through life I have suffered
My heart now is stone, my body is
strengthened,
by secrets untold.
Sexism!
Racism!
These will not last.
I've found my identity
revealed in the past.

I am a Blackwoman of this I can boast.
No need to be knocked from pillar to post.

The reason I'm writing I think you shoud know
Because we have a future
We've somewhere to go.
So to every Blackwoman who has any doubt
This is the time to shout.

I am a Blackwoman — I am what I am.

QAISRA SHAHRAZ

I left Pakistan for England 20 years ago. I am presently working as a lecturer in a Community College.

I have been writing since I was 14 and my work has been published in She *magazine;* Holding Out; What Big Eyes *you've got.*

Mainly my work explores the fate of young Pakistani Muslim women. Aside from short stories I have written a television play and a children's novel.

NEW SPHERES, NEW HORIZONS. 'NIA ZINDAGI, NYA JEVAN'

It was a Sunday afternoon, and as usual Terminal 3 at Heathrow airport was very busy. In the waiting lounge, families, couples, single men and women were gathered and waiting for their flights to various parts of Africa and Asia.

Amongst the crowd of people, stood one Pakistani family of five. The father was busy checking that the label tags were fixed in their places on his elder daughter, Laila's shoulder bags. Laila was going to Pakistan. She stood looking awkwardly at her mother. She knew exactly how her mother was feeling. They were very close and the parting was very painful for both of them. Her brother and sister, both younger than her kept giving her surreptitious glances. They didn't know how to react or what to do with themselves, standing there in the middle of the lounge, knowing that every minute was precious. They felt very miserable.

Their father glanced on the lounge wall clock and addressed his elder daughter, 'Time to go, I am afraid. Otherwise you'll miss your flight, Laila.'

'Already?' his wife asked, giving him a sharp glance. Time was passing by too quickly for her liking.

'Check and see if you've got everything with you.' she told Laila.

Laila browsed through her shoulder bag. Everything was there: her ticket, her passport, her travel vouchers and her gold jewellery.

'Don't forget to write to us, Baji, and phone us if you can,' her brother reminded her.

'Yes, I will as soon as I reach Lahore.' she replied.

'And don't worry about anything. You are going to your home.'

Laila nodded absently and mumbled. 'Accha — yes.' She had heard that statement so many times in the last month or so.

She glanced at the clock. Yes she must go, yet she didn't want to leave them. Her father came to her rescue. He signalled her to go. She embraced her mother first of all, and then turned to her father. He kissed the top of her head and gave her a reassuring pat.

'Goodbye Baji,' her sister Farah, hugged her uninhibitedly, knowing that her sister was actually going now. Her brother, Sarfraz did the same.

Picking up her two bags, Laila gave them a last expressive glance and turned to go.

The other four watched her go until she disappeared from sight amidst the flurry of other passengers. Disconsolately they retraced their way out of the airport. Fifteen minutes later their car raced away on the motorway to Leeds. It was a silent journey. No one felt inclined towards conversation. They were lost in their own thoughts concerning Laila. It seemed as if their family was halved. The parents were very close to their daughter. They would miss her dreadfully. God knew when they would see her again. Life would never be the same without her.

Laila queued behind the other passengers as their bags were checked by the security officers. With the checking over, they entered the departure lounge. Laila sat on one of the smart looking chairs dotted round the room. Her eye caught the phone box. Perhaps she could make a quick phone call to her friends in Leeds. She knew her family would just have got onto the motorway. She felt an ache at the thought of her family. She was missing them already. No! She didn't want to think about them yet. She would have plenty of time to do that during her journey. She didn't quite feel inclined to phone her friends. They seemed so far away and part of another world, a world from which she had divorced herself since yesterday evening.

She turned towards the family who were sitting nearby. They were probably going to spend their Christmas holidays in Pakistan, and to visit their relatives and friends. She smiled to herself. She remembered the time when three years earlier she and her family had gone to Pakistan altogether. It was then that she'd met Rashad....

She switched her thoughts to the present. She

didn't want to think of 'him' or 'them' yet. She smiled at the little boy sitting next to her, dressed in his best three piece suit.

'Hello! What's your name?' she asked in English.

'Usman,' he relied shyly.

'Are you going to Pakistan?' his mother ventured in Urdu.

'Ge-Ha Meh Lahore Ja rhi Hue', 'Yes I am going to Lahore', Laila relied in Urdu.

'Are you travelling alone?'

'Yes.'

'Going to visit your relatives?'

'Yes, but actually I am going to visit my in-laws. They live in Pakistan.'

'Did you get married in Pakistan or here?' the woman persisted in asking. This was an interesting case.

'I got married in Leeds about a year ago.'

'And your husband, where is he?'

'He's in Pakistan. he came and stayed in England for a few months, but he didn't like England very much. He has a super job in Lahore. So he returned about three months ago.'

'So now, you are going to join him, to settle there?'

'Yes,' Laila answered quietly. It still hadn't quite registered in her mind and heart that she was leaving England and settling in Pakistan for good. She still liked to believe that she was going for a holiday, just like the last time. She would stay there for a few months and then return to her everyday life in England.

Passengers, mainly Pakistanis, were getting up to go. Laila picked her bags and joined the queue. Ten minutes later Laila was comfortably seated on the plane. She sat on her own. She was lucky that no one sat next to her, least of all a man. She would have felt very uneasy.

She tied her seat belt and listened mechanically to the air stewardess' instructions on inflatable life jackets and what to do in case of emergency. She looked out of the small jet window. The plane was rising higher and higher into the air. Heathrow airport and London was receding into the distance, as the plane mingled with the cottony clouds over the English Channel.

Laila looked away. It was finally goodbye. She had left the old Laila behind, and in her place sat a stranger. She settled back in her seat and let the day's events roll before her eyes. Until this moment she had clung to the belief that the future was far away. It hadn't quite sunk in that she was actually going to live in another country, away from her family, friends, city, country and a way of life that was second nature to her, and one which she had grown to love. She had spent the last fifteen years of her life in Leeds. When she first came to England with her parents she was eight years old, and thus her early development years were spent in an English enviroment.

What was troubling her now and what had bothered her from the beginning, once she realised that she might have to settle in Pakistan for good, was the thought of whether she would fit in with the life there, with Rashad's family. She had been to Pakistan three times before and she had loved every minute of it. She had stayed with Rashad's family for three days. She was touched by their kindness, their gaiety, their hospitality, and on the whole everything about the household had appealed to her. She'd taken to them.

Now on reflection, she argued with herself, then it was a holiday. It's different from being a guest to a permanent member of a household. And naturally, just as her view of them had altered, so too will they be seeing her in a new light. As a bride, a daughter-in-law, a sister-in-law, and a permanent member of the household, and they would have to adjust their views accordingly.

As she was the product of a different environment, another culture and society she was likely to be scrutinised down to the minutest details. She was well familiar with the cliche-ridden and stereotyped views that some people in Pakistan held about Muslim Pakistani girls being brought up in the 'decadent' West. They were said to have too much freedom and were likely to have imbibed the immoral and permissive ways of Western society.

It was not only a matter of combatting the ingrained prejudices that the people held over there, it was also a matter of her own prejudices, and fears. The overwhelming fear that prevailed over her the last few days was whether she would happily fit into the ways of her husband's household. On her last visit to Pakistan, she had tasted the feelings of being an outsider. There were odd occasions when she had felt quite isolated, because she could not communicate on the same level with her two cousins. And yet they happened to be of her own age. She felt very awkward, for she had nothing in common with them or their likes, their interests, their special delight in fashion, music, books, films and the world of glamour in general. Their whole approach to life in general. She might as well have landed from another planet. Her clothes and their style were criticised. She was made to feel gauche. Having come from England, the heart of fashion, so they reckoned, they expected her to be dressed in the height of fashion and her head well groomed in the latest of hair styles.

She had disappointed them. She felt like a country mouse set loose amongst city ones. They had wanted to display her, to show her off to their friends — as 'their cousin from England', but she didn't fit the bill. She failed to impress upon them that she really wasn't interested in fashion in the same way as they were, nor did it matter a great deal to her. Soon however, they were showing her a thing or two. How she should style her hair, the angle at which she should drape her *Duppata,* not around her shoulders, but on one side, draping freely downwards, and how she should wear the *Kohl* in her eyes.

Ironically before she knew these two cousins, one of whom, Najma, who was now her sister-in-law, she had hardly been fashion-conscious. Since her return to England she began to take a keen interest in creating a colourful and glamorous wardrobe, consisting of matching *Shalwar — Kameze — Dupatta suits and saris* of all colours and patterns. She had of course changed with time. Instead of a budding teenager, she was now a woman of twenty three years of age.

Her hand crept to her hair, and she peered forward into the plane window to catch a glimpse of herself. Her new hairstyle suited her. It framed her face nicely, and made her look very young. She had it layered, permed and streaked in auburn highlights. She took a satisfied glance at herself. The chiffon *Dupatta* that she was wearing had cost her a lot of money. She had asked a friend of hers who had done a fashion design course at the polytechnic to design the suit for her. If first appearances were in question, then she had done her best to appear attractive and elegant, not gauche as the last time. She probably would be welcomed with open arms in the fashion-ridden, well-to-do society of Gulberg, in Lahore.

The air hostess wheeled the food trolley up the aisle, handing trays of food to the passengers. Laila pulled down the tray- table. She was handed a tray.

'Chaiy ya kafay?' the air hostess asked.

'Tea please,' Laila replied. But she quickly amended in Urdu, 'Chaiy sukria.'

The Pakistani influence and the Urdu language was already making its impression. The air hostess moved on, persumably to return later.

Laila examined the contents of the tray. The smell of *pilau* rice and *cheema*, with a piece of *nan* made her feel very hungry.

The hostess returned with a pot of tea. Laila held up her plastic cup and smiled.

'Are you travelling alone?' the hostess asked in English. She had learnt from Laila's 'tea please' that this girl was British bred.

'Yes.'

'Visiting?'

'Visiting and perhaps settling for good in Pakistan.'

'Are you married?'

'I am going to join my husband.'

The hostess laughed.

'We bring and take passengers to and fro, including brides, fiances and fiancees. Normally it is brides joining their husbands in England. But now there seems to be a new trend with brides from England, joining their husbands in Pakistan. 'See you later,' she finished, as she moved ahead with her pot of tea.

Laila returned to her dinner with a new thought in her head. Her own mother, with her young two children was one of those wives, who had a long time ago come to England to join her husband. Although she had heard her mother talk about it, she had never until now appreciated what her mother must have felt and experienced as she come to settle in England. To be confronted with an alien land, a different race of people, a different climate, a different culture, a different way of life, and worst of all to the English language, which proved an insurmountable barrier. She had no relatives, no friends, and unable to speak the language, she couldn't communicate with her English neighbours. It was only later, as she picked up the English vocabulary and learnt to speak English fluently in a women's English class, that she began to build up a happy life, and was full of confidence. She could do the shopping, speak to her neighbours, talk to her children's teachers. Like a flower, she opened out and hungrily absorbed what she had missed out on in the early years.

At least, she, Laila, could identify with Pakistan. She had been born in Lahore and spent the first seven years of her life there. She knew the people of the land, its culture and its language, and therefore her predicament was different from her mother's. Loneliness that her mother had experienced in the early years, was something she hoped and knew she would never suffer from, once she was ensconced in her in-laws household. Personally she had no desires of wanting to set up her own home with her husband. If she got on well with her mother-in-law and the other members of the household, then she had no reason to live separately. Although she didn't have a great deal in common with Najma, she liked her for her frivolous and buoyant ways. Anyway she would soon be married herself.

There was no use in denying the fact that she would miss England dreadfully, her family, her friends and of course her job. She had worked as nurserynurse in a local primary school in Leeds. Only last month she had handed in her notice of resignation. Rashad had promised in his last letter to her, that he would find some post, in her line of work, in Lahore. She still wasn't sure, whether he was indulging her, so that she wouldn't feel too bad about leaving her work, and especially as it was because of his work she had to leave England and join him there.

It had been quite a sacrifice, she just hoped Rashad appreciated her gesture. In her heart she knew that her in-laws wouldn't really approve of her working, earning her living as they would see it, as according to their way of thinking and class, it was an insult for a woman to work, unless it was a high status post, that of a lecturer, doctor or a lawyer. It was the husband's prerogative to provide for his wife's keep. Education was a highly valued asset for a young woman, but it wasn't as it was in England, a passport for work. Najma, who had just completed her first year of MA at the Punjab University, typical of her class had no particular desire to work. Why should she work? She was probably going to be married into a wealthy and well-to-do family like her own. Still quite hopeful, Laila had packed a pile of children's books and some brochures of children's games and toys with the rest of her luggage. She nourished a longing to open and design a nursery in Lahore, stocked and styled even better than any in Leeds.

With her meal finished she moved the tray aside and waited for the air steward to collect it. She settled back in her seat and closed her eyes, wanting to catch up on some sleep. Last night she had only slept for a couple of hours. With a four hours' difference between Pakistan time and that of England, she probably would feel disorientated for a day or two. Anyway she knew from her previous visit, that a day or two was spent in talking, meeting and staying up well after midnight.

Sleep caught up with Laila, she turned her face towards the window. She didn't want anyone walking up and down the aisle staring into her sleeping face. She didn't notice when the air steward collected the tray.

The next time Laila woke up was when the plane landed at Dubai airport to pick up passengers and to refuel. Most of the new passengers getting on the plane from Dubai were Pakistani men, working in Dubai and going home for their annual or half yearly holidays. They were laden with electrical goods, tape recorders and videos — presents to give to their families, relatives or friends.

The seat beside Laila remained empty, until a plump middle-aged Pakistani woman decided to sit there. The men had passed by, not wanting to sit next to an unattached lady. The Muslim values and conventions were already beginning to have their impact. If it was in England, on a train or on a bus, anybody, man or woman, would have sat beside her and she wouldn't have minded. Here, now, with her mind attuned to Muslim values she would have been highly surprised if a young man had sat in the seat next to her. It would be a very uncomfortable journey.

Laila smiled at the woman sitting besides her, and addressed a greeting.

'Assalama — alaikum.'

'Wa Laikum salam,' the woman replied, 'Tuh London to aiye ho,' speaking in Punjabi.

'Jee, meh London to aiye huen,' she answered in the same language. Yes, she came from London. London being short for England. The woman's dark eyes swept over Laila's head in understanding. She looked a 'London Miss' alright. Laila returned the glance. The woman wore a black bulbous looking cloak, the veil covering her entire ample body and head, popularly worn by the Eastern women. Seeing Laila looking at her, she drew the *chador* around her, and straightened the piece covering her head.

'This *hijab* is better than the fashionably styled *burqa* worn by Pakistani women, which shows each and every curve of the woman's body. I bought this from a bazaar in Dubai.' She explained to Laila. 'Mind you, not that many women seem to wear burqa in Pakistan these days. They seem to prefer the *Chador*. It's only elder women like myself who end up wearing the *chador* and the *burqa*. And some young women don't even wear the *chador*. They go around with rope-like *dupattas* round their necks. If they are not going to drape it round their shoulders and over their heads in a proper fashion they might as well not wear them. I suppose in London you don't wear *dupattas* or *burqas* .' She finished.

'We wear *dupattas* of course, most of the time, as part of our everyday wear, but not *burqas*. Instead we wear coats and jackets. It's quite cold there most of the year, and also they cover the body quite modestly,' she explained in justification, and asked, 'Are you travelling alone?'

'Yes, I went to visit my son and his family in Dubai. He works in a tractor company.'

'Is your family with you?'

'No, I am travelling alone.'

From there on one explanation led to another. The last three hours of her journey passed very quickly. Laila talked about her family, about life in England, about her in-laws. The woman was obviously intrigued and suggested to her that as they were both going to Lahore they travel from Karachi to Lahore together.

She had left a frosty morning in England, and arrived in a hot afternoon in Karachi. As soon as she got off the plane, the hot air swept over her body. As she was driven to the 'arrivals' lounge, Laila surveyed the scene around her. Here she was in Pakistan again. All of a sudden she felt a warm glow inside and a feeling of exhilaration washed over her. It was good to be back!

The same scene met her eyes. Instead of fair faces, there were brown ones, the women in their traditional *shalwar — kameze suits,* porters hurrying to help with luggage, huge potted plants dotted round the large, bright and airy lounge, the purring noise of the air conditioners and the fan, the mosaic work on the polished marble floor. Laila followed the older woman, through the customs. The latter had taken her under her wing. Their flight to Lahore was due in another hour. Laila looked at her watch. It still showed British time. Her family in Leeds would be just getting up. Her brother and sister getting ready to go to their schools. How far away they seemed now. She didn't want to think of them. Too much was happening to her, too many scenes racing before her eyes. Later in the confines of her room, she would think of them.

Knowing where the ladies' room was, she went to freshen up. She wanted to look her best. She would be seeing them in less than two hours. She couldn't wait to see Rashad. In Leeds, he had seemed so far away, now that she was in Pakistan she was impatient to see him.

In the cool afternoon of Lahore, a crowd of people waited in the arrivals open courtyard, under the shades of the verandas. They were all waiting for the arrival of the domestic flight from Karachi. Amongst the crowd of people were Laila's in-laws and her husband. Her mother-in-law, Akhtar Begum, Najma and her brother- in-law, Firdaus, and Rashad were all waiting impatiently for the plane to arrive, which was due any minute now. All of them were lost in their own thoughts concerning Laila's arrival. It would mark a change in their present life style. They all hoped the change was for the better.

Rashad fervently believed so. He was desperately waiting to catch a glimpse of his wife. He had counted each day of the three months he had spent away from her. Although he was eager to leave England, later he regretted having done so. At least he would have been with her. Not that he had enjoyed his stay in England very much. It was alright for a holiday but not for life. Compared to the gay evening life he was accustomed to in Lahore, he found life in Leeds very dull. He had no friends, and there was no prospect of a good job. After three years of climbing the ladder to gain his present post in Pakistan, he couldn't stomach the idea of working in a warehouse, wheeling boxes around, and being under someone's thumb all the time. He had too much pride to accept that fate willingly.

He was acutely aware of what his wife must be feeling, after parting from her parents, brother and sister and her fears about coming to settle here. Just as England didn't suit him or appeal to him, perhaps she wouldn't like it here in Pakistan. He fully appreciated that she was coming to Pakistan for his sake and left her job for his job. He had already made enquires in the private sector of primary education in Lahore. He was optimistic that some institution would be very happy to make use of Laila's talent and experience.

He had taken a month's leave and charted out a month of visits and engagements. He hoped they would completely take Laila's mind off England. If she felt homesick and missed England very much, he would arrange to take a summer's leave and visit England and Greece. He had some very good Greek friends.

'There's the plane!' Najma shouted excitedly

as she spotted the plane first. They all looked up and waited expectantly. Five minutes later the plane had landed on the runway and stood still. Soon the passengers began to leave the plane.

Laila's family looked carefully, trying to spot her in the crowd of passengers walking towards the arrivals' lounge.

Rashad's mother was the first to spot Laila — she had noticed her walk. In one glance she had drunk in her daughter-in-law's appearance. She wasn't displeased. Thank goodness she was here safe and sound!

Laila followed behind the woman from Dubai into the arrivals lounge and waited to collect her luggage. Her heart was beating wildly. Any minute now she would see Rashad and his family.

With her luggage safe on the trolley and having said her goodbye to the woman from Dubai, Laila stepped out of the lounge and walked up to the people waiting outside.

Out of the sea of faces confronting her, she caught Rashad's glance and she held her breath. She had forgotten how good looking he was. A shy smile played over her features. His eyes were already transmitting silent messages over the heads of the others. Laila looked away reluctantly and her eyes encompassed the other three members of her husband's family. She smiled and went to meet them, greeting with *assalama — alaikum*. Her father-in-law wasn't there she noticed.

Rashad drew forward and took the luggage from the porter following in Laila's footsteps. Akhtar Begum walked up to her daughter-in-law and hugged her affectionately. 'Welcome home daughter' she said. Then Najma kissed Laila on the cheek. English people's custom of kissing their wives in public didn't apply to her people. A low hello, a reassuring smile, and a silent message via the eyes was the chief form of communication between herself and her husband.

Rashad guided her to their waiting car. Soon they left the airport behind and the car sped along the wide, conifer lined road one of the most exclusive suburban areas in Lahore, Gulberg. This was the district populated by the upper middle classes, with their huge and ornately styled *kothis*. Some other relatives of Laila's family lived in the old city of Lahore, the heavily populated and not so prosperous area. For Laila, from England for the last time, she didn't quite feel at home in it. It was too 'posh' as she told her friends in Leeds, too class-ridden. It had codes and ethics and the inhabitants lived by them, dressed by them. In fact their whole life style was dictated by them. It was in the traditional teeming bazaars of Lahore that Laila truly felt happy. For her that was Pakistan.

Next morning Laila got up feeling at odds with her surrounding. This wasn't her bedroom. She was thinking of her cosy room in Leeds, with its single teak wardrobe and matching dressing table unit, a bookcase and a desk and chair.

She opened her eyes fully and surveyed the large bedroom in which she slept on a king sized bed. Its intricately designed walnut mahogany headboard matched the rest of the furnishing, consisting of fitted high-ceiling double wardrobes, vanity unit, bookcase, display unit and bedside cabinets. As was the normal practice in Pakistan, the furniture was designed to order by local craftsmen.

Laila turned on her side. Rashad had gone. The dent remained in his pillow. She smiled to herself. She stepped out of the bed. The cool marble floor sent a shiver up her spine. There were doors dotted around the room. One of them led to the adjoining bathroom and shower room. The villa was designed in such a way that each bedroom was fitted with a bathroom and a shower. This was luxury indeed. No more queuing up outside the bathroom and loo door as in Leeds.

Laila was towel drying her hair, when there was a knock on the door. Next minute Najma entered, all smiles. 'Brother Rashad's been up for some time now. We didn't want to disturb you.' She ended, coming to stand behind Laila who was sitting on the vanity stool.

She looked at Laila's and her own reflection in the large oval mirror and mentally noted the comparison. Laila understood Najma's look. With her own face bare of make-up and hair wound up in a turban fashion and a plain pink *Kurtha*, she was no match for the glossy, out of the magazine image that Najma presented in the mirror. Down to the well manicured painted toe nails and the matching hairgrips daintily wound in her hair, Najma had the appearance of a professional fashion model. Noting the complacent look on Najma's face, the illusion wasn't lost on the latter.

'What were you thinking of wearing?' Najma enquired, taking the towel from Laila's hand and rubbing it gently against her hair. It was the custom for a sister-in-law to see to the needs of a new bride. She fingered the deep auburn layers appreciatively. Apparently Laila had gone to a very good beauty salon Najma thought, little guessing that the latter had gone to a hairdressers at the end of their road.

'I don't know. I haven't thought about it yet—?'

'You see as far as we are concerned, you are a bride, who has come to our home for the first time.' With a twinkle Najma's eyes skirted the bed suggestively. Laila felt her cheeks blush hotly. She had been married for six months, yet this morning she felt as if she was newly married, and in a way she was, she reflected as far as her in-law family was concerned.

Najma walked up to one of the wardrobes and with a flourish opened its doors, to reveal an array of outfits hanging on hangers. She drew out a heavy, bulky looking outfit in red, and gently laid it on the bed, opening it out for Laila to see.

'This is your *shahrara* that we had made for you as a present.'

Laila marvelled at the intricate sequin work on the tunic's neckline, on the edge on the sleeves, and on the bottom half of the *shahrara*. To complete the outfit there was a red cobweb type chiffon *dupatta* with a similar sequin and bead design, but this time in the shape of a butterfly. Red was the customary bright colour, reminiscent of youth and life, worn by the brides of the sub-continent of India. At her registration in a Leeds office, she wore a white sari, and later at the Muslim *nikkah* and reception, she wore a red embroiderd *sari*.

Out of a locked compartment inside the wardrobe Najma drew out a number of velvety-looking cases in all shapes. Laila recognised them as jewellery cases. Before her silent gaze Najma opened each case and laid them out in a line on the bed. The glittery gold jewellery studded with stones of various kinds, sources, shapes and sizes stared at Laila. There was a choker necklace, designed to embrace the neck, a heart shaped locket, to be worn on casual occasions, and a long dangling 3-layered necklet. There were three pairs of *Kanteh, chumkah* and a pair of studs. In a deep square shaped case there was a dozen delicately designed gold bangles. In another large case was a *panjagla* . The whole piece was held together by a bracelet.

'Everything is so beautiful,' Laila spoke in awe. Her own ornaments from England consisted of one such gold jewellery set and a dozen colourful accessories from Chelsea Girl, chunky bracelets, bead necklaces and matching ear studs.

'Chose whatever you like to wear from these cases, but do try to look your best, as we are expecting a lot of guests today. I'll go and see if your breakfast is ready.'

She left Laila to dress. While she dressed Laila recalled moments from the previous night. A flurry of movements, sea of faces, embraces and hugs and kisses from every female quarter, and polite chatter, 'How are you? How is your family in England? How was your journey... '

It was all so strange and unreal surrounded by a huge room full of people of all ages. Some she recognised as relatives, others as their close friends or neighbours, all of whom had come to welcome her home. Her jaws ached from smiling at them. In turn she was scrutinised from her head to her toes peeping out of her sandals. They were all dressed in all styles of clothing. Her eyes moved from the Turkish hat that her father-in-law wore, to the Levi's worn by her brother-in-law, to the sensuous folds of Najma's sari, to the hand embroidered lace of her mother-in-law's *dupatta*.

Aware of her fatigue and how mind boggling it was to travel from one country to another, from

one environment to another, Akhtar Begum ex-
cused her daughter-in-law's absence and took
her to her room. She remembered her own experience when she went to perform *hajj*
pilgrimage in Saudi Arabia, and that was a
Muslim country and still she felt an alien. Rashad
joined her much later. She remembered falling
asleep with the voice of the Muezzin's prayer
from the mosque ringing in her ears.

Laila stared critically at her reflection in the
mirror. She looked quite lovely, but then so did
every bride dressed in all her finery. This time
she was dressed for the benefit of people here
in Lahore, Rashad's relatives and friends. They
would want to see the new bride and so they
must be indulged accordingly. A glance at the
contents of the wardrobe had told her how much
her mother-in-law had spent on her trousseau.

Lifting the folds of the *shahrara* in her hand
and draping the *dupatta* around her shoulders
and head Laila let herself out of the room. Luckily
she remembered where the dining room was
located.

'Assalama alaikum', she said on entering.
Mother and daughter sat on the couch in one
corner of the room. They looked up. Akhtar
Begum smiled in welcome 'wa laikum salam', and
beckoned her to come further into the room
'You look lovely! Let me have a good look at you.'
Laila stood before her mother-in-law. The latter
drew the *dupatta* aside and looked at Laila's

throat. 'Yes, just as I thought. The choker suits you.' she nodded her head in satisfaction.

Najma got up and led Laila to the heavily laden dining table, apparently laid for her benefit. There was *halwa pourri, chana mathiey,* boiled eggs, toast, biscuits and pastries of all types. With a phobia against fatty and sugary things Laila felt quite nauseated as she stared at everything. Nothing would induce her to try the *pourris* fried in *ghee.* From habit she reached for the toast.

Laila was delighted when that same evening, her friend Farah, from Leeds, now married and living in Lahore, came to visit her. It was Farah initially who had encouraged Laila to come and settle in Pakistan, for she herself was very happy there. While on holiday in Leeds last year she had talked to Laila about her life in Lahore, and later had continued to write, from Pakistan. She was accompanied by her mother-in-law, who sat and talked with Akhtar Begum.

Laila stared at her friend. In appearance, Farah was the epitome of a well-to-do young society woman, who hadn't a care in the world. Her two children were left in the care of her sister-in-law. From the beginning she spoke in English. She asked Laila all about Leeds, about her family and her other friends. She enlarged upon her own life, her in-laws, her way of life and how very happy she was with her lot. She wouldn't consider returning to England apart from holidays.

'Can you imagine it, we go on international

tours once a year, the children are looked after by my in-laws. All the housework is done by the servants. All I have to do is some cooking and even that is shared. My in-laws are very good to me. In fact they have pampered me. In the evenings we go for *Sehr,* to the cinemas, drama shows, or go out shopping. What is there for me in England. I'd probably be living in some crummy sort of terraced house, locked in by the cold, minding the children, as well as working, cooking, washing and cleaning. There would be no time for me. Here I lead a life of leisure.'

'Don't you miss your family, your friends in England? I am missing mine terribly, already.'

'Of course, I do, but I go and visit them almost every summer. I don't miss them so much now. I've got used living here now., I feel a stranger in England. Mind you, I'll tell you what I miss - soaps, like Coronation Street and Dallas. Is that still on?'

'Yes.'

'And also not being able to speak English all the time. You don't know how happy I feel in speaking English with you. I haven't got an accent, have I?'

Laila Laughed.

'No! But my own Urdu is a bit rusty. I am glad I did an 'O' level in it. It has helped.'

They chatted for over two hours, during which time they had tea and some other people came to visit Laila. Laila felt very relaxed after Farah's visit. The latter had put her mind at rest. She promised to visit her later. She lived in a neighbouring suburb, Shadman, Farah was obviously impressed by Laila's new home and its surroundings.

Laila later in the confines of her room got ready to say her evening prayer. She had discovered that her in-laws's family were very strict where prayers were concerned. Her mind dwelt on the conversation she had had, with Farah. Her friend was obviously very happy and had no inclination to pursue a career of any sort. Would that apply to her? Would she gradually become another Farah? Would she be statisfied in sitting around, dolling herself up, visiting places or people, or entertaining others? Her mind couldn't quite visualise that predicament. Rashad had promised! She must talk to him about it. At peace with herself, she prostrated herself on the prayer rug and concentrated on her prayers.

Three weeks later, Laila was sitting in the beautiful marbled courtyard, lined with earthen pots of various species of plants. She was reminiscencing over what she had been doing over the last three weeks. She had visited three private nurseries and some primary schools, and spoken to some of the teachers and head teachers. She had inspected their surroundings carefully and mentally noted their provision, the toys, the play areas, the books, physical education apparatus and other items.

She had held lengthy discussions with her parents-in-law and with Rashad about her plans. After their initial hesitation, they became quite enthusiastic about what she had to suggest. In fact, they revelled in an enterprising daughter-in-law. It was decided that as well as setting up a new nursery, herself, in Lahore, Laila, with the help of her husband, ought to open up a business in one of the most sought after shopping arcades under the title 'Play and Learn', and all relevant child-centred goods would be imported from England and America. She had already written off to various firms and companies. She phoned her parents in Leeds to send her more brochures and keep her up to date with children's book publications. Parents who lived in Gulberg and other wealthy suburbs were very keen on purchasing the best of products for their children's education. Therefore her ideas would sell. Her mind was buzzing with potential ideas and plans. She couldn't wait to get started. The next few months would be taken up in buying the necessary land, designing the nursery with an architect, and then furnishing it appropriately. Then advertising it, as well as employing staff to run it and she was playing the central role in it. It would be the best, in fact better than any in Leeds.

She leaned back in the wicker chair and sipped a glass of mango juice. The future looked very rosy. What would she be doing now in

England, in Leeds, at this moment. Probably mixing pots of paints, shepherding children into the wash rooms, putting on their aprons, reading a story to them and constantly at the beck and call of the nursery teacher. Her mind recoiled from the picture. She wouldn't go back to that situation for anything. Perhaps, like Farah, Pakistan after all had a lot to offer her.

Already day by day England seemed to have become so remote. She lived a very busy and eventful life and had no time to think about England. Even the voices of her brother, sister and her family seemed so alien to her ears. They were part of a world which she had well and truly left behind, and now she didn't regret leaving it at all. At least nobody made racist remarks here and called her 'Paki'.

She got up and straightened the folds of her chiffon *sari*. She must go and check her wardrobe, and see what she was going to wear during the next few days. They were going on holiday to Murree, a mountainous resort. They were leaving early in the morning.

THE ELOPEMENT

The telephone was ringing again. The three women in the living room jumped visibly. They exchanged quick glances, silent messages transmitted from the eyes travelled to and fro.

No one spoke.

The phone began to ring persistently. Two pairs of eyes turned to one figure seated by the window.

Suriya Qureshi encompassed her two teenage daughters in one glance, noting their nervous movements. Apparently they didn't know what to do. They were waiting for a sign from her. Waiting to see whether she would get up and answer the phone herself.

She disappointed them. By the nod of her head she motioned her youngest daughter, Farina. Out of her three daughters she was the good conversationalist. She could cope with any situation. Farina, however, drew further into the settee and nudged her elder sister Nadia.

'You go,' she hissed.

Nadia got up very reluctantly, stepping on her sister's feet as she made a dash for the door and disappeared into the hallway.

In the living room mother and daughter stared at one another, their hearts literally in their mouths, their ears cocked to the conversation going on over the telephone.

In both heads the same thought hammered. Was it *her*? They waited, trying to glean their information from the nuances of words and phrases that Nadia was using. The mother's head fell back against the sofa.

It was not *her*. It was not Rubiya. Nadia would not be speaking to her like that. Her words were too polite and stilted. It sounded as if she was speaking to her aunt Jamila. Not her again. Did she hear correctly? Or was it her imagination? Nadia was talking about Rubiya. Surely Jamila had not found out about Rubiya — surely not. Oh God! she could not bear it. She felt faint. Her heart was beating rapidly.

'I bet she has found out, and is now trying to find something out from Nadia. She is very good at doing that. Oh God, why did not I answer the phone and shut her up. Surely Nadia hadn't gone mad and blabbed out the truth.' Suriya for a moment did not realise that she was speaking out her thoughts. Only when she looked at her daughter did she realise that she was speaking out loudly.

She ignored her daughter. She must do something. She must call Nadia and herself have a word with Jamila. Just as she got up from her seat she heard the clicking sound of the phone, as Nadia replaced the receiver on its cradle. Too late.

Nadia entered.

Two pairs of eyes turned towards her, scanning her face quickly for any tell-tale expression it might betray. She gave her mother and sister a watery smile, knowing too well what they were thinking about. She came further into the room and sat down gingerly in the vacant place beside her sister. She addressed her mother.

'It was aunt Jamila. She wanted to know whether Rubiya would sew for her a *Shalwar Kameze* suit...'

'What did you say?' Suriya interrupted her daughter quickly.

'I told her that Rubiya was out, visiting a friend of hers. Therefore she could not say whether she was able to or not. She then added that she would drop in later this evening or tomorrow afternoon with the suit.'

Nadia exchanged a significant glance with her mother.

Suriya's heart sank. Oh God, Jamila on top of everything else. She feared this sister-in-law as she did no other person, excepting her husband. Jamila, with her eagle eyes and her sharp mind she was sure to find out the truth. They could not lie to her — not to her. She was sure the horrible truth was written on their faces. Jamila would sense immediately that something was amiss. In fact everything was amiss. They were not the same, their thoughts and actions weren't the same. It seemed that since yesterday afternoon they had entered another world, a theatre in which they themselves were strangers, puppets in fact, with Rubiya as the puppeteer.

She still marvelled at the fact that her husband had not found out. It was a sheer miracle that Haji Farook Din did not know that his elder daughter, Rubiya had not been seen in the house since yesterday morning. He had no idea that she had left home and eloped with a young man, God knew where to. A two minute telephone call from a phone box yesterday evening gave them the most hateful, the most shocking and shameful information. She was going away with this man, and that was all they needed to know. Suriya Qureshi and her two daughters had reeled with shock.

When the phone call had come, Haji Farook was not in. Nor was he in when Farina had rushed in with the unbelievable news that she had seen Rubiya getting into a car with a strange man and drive off without saying anything. Farina omitted to say that she had seen the man with Rubiya before. At breakfast time Haji Farook had not commented on his daughter's absence. He probably thought that she was upstairs somewhere or still asleep. It would not have occurred to him in a thousand years that his eldest daughter was missing — that she had not slept in her bed, but was out there in the night with some young man, God knew where. Her mind revolted from the picture of this man.

Why the news would kill her husband. He would never recover from the shock. What had happened to the father of that disgraceful affair they had heard about last year. The father long after the affair was over, was in and out of hospital. Haji Farook would never be able to hold his head upright in public, in their community, amongst their relatives and friends.

Had she herself not died a thousand deaths since yesterday afternoon? She could not still believe that this was happening to her, to them. It could not be. What had they done to deserve this? It was an unreal world she had entered since Farina came with the damning news. It was a long nightmare, from which she must wake up. Oh, *Allah Pak,* she must. It had to be a nightmare. In a few seconds her complacent, happy and respectable — oh so respectable world had toppled, to be replaced by this shame and nightmare. Her daughter, surely, could not do this to them. She could not be so cruel and so shameful. They did not deserve this treatment. Her father a Haji too! Shame on her!

They had heard of such an incident sometime ago. But they had shuffled it aside in their minds. It had no relevance for them. Shame and filth was attached to this incident. Theirs was a respectable family. And both the parents could not conceive any of their daughters committing that shameful crime. They'd felt sorry for the parents who had to suffer the consequences of their daughter's crime. Suriya recalled with bitterness the twist of fate. Once they had pitied those parents, now they were to be pitied. She couldn't bear the thought. How would she show her face amongst her friends? What had Rubiya done?

Suriya closed her eyes in anguish, breathing heavily, her body was rocked by silent sobs. She drew her *dupatta* over her face, in order to hide it from her two daughters watching each and every movement of hers. Rubiya had thrown it all away. Her reputation, her parents', her honour, her *izzat* and theirs, all at one go. What had she done? Again Suriya found it hard to believe that her daughter had left home, perhaps for good and committed that heinous crime. The images it conjured up in her mind left her feeling nauseous. Again the injustice of it all struck her. Every fibre, every cell of her being loathed her daughter. She had no right to cause such suffering in their household, to cause such havoc in their lives.

At the moment only she and her two daughters knew about this. She daren't think what would happen if her husband found out or any of their relatives, especially Jamila, who would never allow them to recover from the incident. On the contrary she would gloatingly force her point home — 'This is what happened if you gave your daughters too much freedom and let them become too Westernised.' Suriya closed her eyes tightly — wanting to shut out the picture of the world outside. She'd never be ready to confront the world outside.

For how long could the three of them hide the truth from her husband and other people. Jamila said she was coming and she was bound to find out that Rubiya was not to be seen anywhere. Already one day had passed. This afternoon had given her a taste of what her ordeal was going to be like if Rubiya did not return. The sudden appearance of one of Rubiya's friends had thrown the three into jitters, so that they had to resort to excuses and lies. All the time they'd felt guilty at guarding their shameful secret. It was the most trying moment of their lives. They fidgeted with their rings, their hair, their bangles and their clothes, hardly paying any attention to what Rubiya's friend, Neelum was saying. Their thoughts were with Rubiya and the telephone. Their monosyllabic replies were very stilted. The girls were sure that their own nervousness would arouse suspicion. They wished their visitor gone and the time to pass quickly.

Even amongst themselves the subject of Rubiya's elopement was a taboo. It was too terrible to discuss openly. Farina and Nadia were unable to voice their thoughts openly. Both of them condemmed their sister's action. 'How could she do it?' they queried. 'Had she taken leave of her senses? Did she feel no *sharm*?' They shuddered at the thought of their sister being in close proximity with a strange man. They tried to put themselves in her place and imagine what she felt and what must have compelled her to do what she did. Their minds, however shied away from the situation. They knew the man Rubiya was infatuated with. There was no other term to describe this relationship. While Rubiya might have described it as 'love', they would have labelled it as infatuation and sheer madness. Although younger than Rubiya they knew their limits. They despised their sister's action in wanting to ape their English girlfriends by having a boyfriend too. It would never work, they were sure. Rubiya was just infatuated and she would return. They would tire of each other soon enough, especially when they couldn't survive in a social vacuum, surrounded by shame and rejection.

Nadia cursed herself over and over again. She was the one to be blamed. She knew what was going on but had done nothing about it. She ought to have warned her mother about it. Now Rubiya was lost forever. Even if she came back, she would carry the stigma, the stain of her action forever. The shameful deed would be labelled on her for eternity. But worst of all she had let her family down. The disgraceful deed would shroud all of them for the rest of their lives. Rubiya and their chances of marriages — well that was another story...

Rubiya had not only slammed the door on her future, but theirs too. Rubiya's elopement would definitely mean that their own freedom to go when and where they pleased would be curtailed. They would be made Rubiya's scapegoats — in fact, made to suffer for *her* crime. Already their mother had lost her trust in them. It was almost as if she expected both of them to do a disappearing act — as if they too would elope any minute. Thinking back, neither of the two sisters had been out of doors since yesterday afternoon.

Worse still, there was going to be social repercussions too. Friends and relatives would be pointing accusing fingers at them - referring to them as sisters of the girl who had committed that horrible crime. They would be in the limelight and each and every action of theirs scrutinised and criticised. If their father found out...

Both of them shuddered at the thought. Why he would never allow them out of their front room door. What had too much freedom brought them? Nothing but shame and disgrace. They would always be the butt of his anger. They felt sorry for their father. He would never be able to lift his head in public. Always he would be surrounded by shame. From a very respectable member of their community he would become the victim of the community's gossip; of their pity for fathering such daughters.

Their mother too was a bag of nerves. She had not eaten or slept since yesterday night. At night she paced the house, keeping her eyes glued to the window pane in case Rubiya turned up. She did not. From nine o'clock this morning she had not left her seat by the window. Her eyes often wandered out, hungry for Rubiya's appearance. If the telephone rang she jumped up in her seat. She did not have the nerve, however, to go and answer it herself. They understood. She would not know what to say to Rubiya, if it was her again. Although her mind and heart cursed Rubiya for what she'd done, every time the phone rang she shrank inwards. She did not want to speak to her. Her mind had already cast her out as her daughter. No love remained in her heart for this daughter. Only a loathing and burning shame, which made her want to curl and shrink in the sofa.

Since yesterday afternoon their house was a shamble. The everyday routine of washing and tidying up was lost. The girls still marvelled at themselves. Despite what they were going through, they managed to cook the evening meal, although in silence, and to act as normal as possible when their father came home for dinner yesterday afternoon and last night. It was not too difficult. After staying with their parents for what they felt was an adequate time so as not to arouse their father's attention, Farina and Nadia escaped to their rooms. At some time or another they had dropped the hint that Rubiya was upstairs in her room. During the rest of the evening they waited nervously in their rooms, expecting any minute for their father to blow his top. Flickng through some paperbacks they waited with their beating hearts until ten o'clock. Everything however appeared normal downstairs. They'd even heard their father laughing at something. They'd felt sorry for their mother's predicament.

When their father actually came upstairs and went to bed, their hearts stood still. They couldn't believe their luck. They sighed with relief. Their father did not know! They marvelled furthermore when their father did not notice Rubiya's absence at breakfast time too, the next morning.

Tonight, however, was going to be different. Their father was bound to notice Rubiya's absence. What if he took it into his head to go and see Rubiya — see how she was doing. They'd earlier dropped a hint about her having a headache or something. Then they would have to tell him the truth. They dreaded that time.

At six o'clock when their father came home, the girls felt very edgy. They did not know what to do with themselves; how to behave; what to say. All they seemed to be doing was exchanging silent glances with one another.

Mother and daughters dreaded the time when their father would mention Rubiya. In Nadia's head, a plan was already forming. If her father wanted to visit Rubiya in her bedroom. Then she'd sleep in Rubiya's bed, and pretend to be her and hope for the best that he wouldn't wake her up if he saw her fast asleep. They'd toyed with their meal not feeling very hungry, but were very much aware of the tension mounting up in the dining room. It was almost tangible; they were sure they could slice their way through it with a knife.

Back in the living room, after the meal and the clearing up in the kitchen, television held no interest for them. Usually Thursday evening found themselves glued to their T.V. set, especially for 'Top of the Pops'. Today, however when their father switched onto another channel, the girls did not bat an eyelid. They'd hardly noticed the prancing figures on the pop stage. Their thoughts were elsewhere. They were busy devising ways of creeping out of the room without arousing their father's interest. Haji Farook, an intelligent and perceptive man, couldn't help but notice their fidgety movements. At one stage in the evening he commented on their noncommittal remarks and monosyllabic rejoinders.

At about nine o'clock he got up and went out of the room. The girls relaxed. When they heard him climb the stairs, they looked at their mother. Fear was etched on her features. They too were afraid. What if he took it into his head to look at Rubiya, they asked themselves.

Nadia got up resolutely. She knew what she was going to do. Her father was in the bathroom. They could tell by the treading of his feet above. Perhaps she still had time to carry out her plan.

She went out of the room.

Suriya heard the backdoor open and then click shut. What was Nadia up to she asked herself. It was not the day for the dustbins to be placed outside. She waited for her to return so that she could ask her this. At the same time she was listening to her husband's footsteps upstairs. Her heart had begun to beat a tattoo again. Her husband's footsteps were now in Rubiya's room.

This was the moment. This was the time they all dreaded. Now the whole world would explode. Suriya shrank inwards — she could not cope with this!

Farina was listening to her father's footsteps too, her eyes staring above at the ceiling.

Neither the mother nor the daughter noticed the living room open and a young woman dressed in outdoor clothes enter the room.

When Suriya caught sight of her, she almost leapt out of her seat. Farina's mouth stood open, unable to believe her eyes. It was almost as if they were watching a Shakespearian play at the Royal Exchange Theatre. 'Rubiya', she whispered the magical word. Surely her eyes were playing tricks on her. For there stood Rubiya, looking worn out and dishevelled. She was apparently struggling to stick a brave and confident expression on her face, but without much success.

Not daring to look at her mother, she addressed her sister.

'I came the back way', she said quietly as if in

explaination of how she got inside the house. She held the key to her sister. As the steps thudded down the stairs, three pairs of eyes turned to the door. Rubiya swivelled a desperate look at her mother. Suriya stared back, her face expressionless. Her mind was already thinking ahead. She'd loathed her daughter, but she was in control once again. She was the puppeteer now, not Rubiya her daughter.

Haji Farook on entering the room, noticed his eldest daughter standing in the middle of the room. A baffled expression settled on his face. He looked at his wife and his youngest daughter, Farina. He returned to look at Rubiya.

'I thought you had a headache. Nadia just told me you were asleep.'

He noticed for the first time the outdoor summer jacket that Rubiya was wearing and the handbag she was clutching to her side. Haji Farook looked at his wife for an answer. Suriya had already decided opon her answer two minutes ago.

'Rubiya went to Jamila's house just before you returned home. Jamila wanted her to sew a *Kameze* for her. Nadia did not know about this. Jamila has just dropped her off....'

'Go to bed child. You look tired. You should not have gone with Jamila if you had a headache.'

With a wave of his hand, Haji Farook dismissed his daughter. Unaware of the charade-like nature of the situation he settled in his seat to await the nine o'clock news on BBC1. Rubiya could not believe her luck. He did not know!

Damn the man! Damn him! her mind cursed. She would never be the same again. She was a fool

Thankfully she made her exit. Her head held high, she muttered her 'Goodnight' to no one in particular. As she left the room she felt her mother's and sister's eyes boring into her back.

LEMN SISSAY

I am a writer and it is my life
I would slit my wrist with a pen not a knife
I am a writer from now until then
My life is my paper, my knife is my pen. ©

I was born in 1967 and lived in Lancashire for
most of my life, now based in Manchester as
a full time writer. My work can be found in
The New British Poetry 1968-88 *(Collins);*
Transformation *(Rivelin Grapheme Press);*
Grass Roots Verse *(Hansib Publications);*
Poetic Licence 1987 *(Commonword Ltd);* The
English File *(B.B.C. Publications).*
   My latest book is Tender Fingers In A
Clenched Fist *(Bogle L'Overture Publication).*
I have recently completed my second play
'No Details' *which will tour from August 1988*
with One Step Theatre Company.

LIVE MAN DIE (CITY SIGH)

Move
Quick
Slick
Time
Tick
Good
Bye
On a
High
Train
Plane
Sun
Rain
Fun
Pain
Be
Sane
Play the
Game
City rain
City pain
Here gone
Quick food
Pass On
Plastic too
Sit to brood
And look at you
Losing time

Meaning
Leaning
On the
Building
Of the
City Sigh
Got to fly
Don't know why
Burger food
Good to spew
To take away
Why not stay
Instead you
People breathe
Bodies seethe
And underneath
Is the
City Sigh
Got to fly
Don't know why
Live man die...

THE RED DEATH OF EDGAR ALLAN POE

He held in his mind the fear
 Of every human fool
    Clown
     Or jack-in-a-box.

He rang the slow bell
    church chime
    death walk
    No crime
    Assasin
In his head so many times...

So many times he
Caressed the barbed wire of his own lines
That chilled his own skin
That bore his own death
Like he haunted himself
With his own breath

He carved his name
Into mountains of depression
And he hastily drank river water
Where the dead sheep lay twitching
Twitching in nervous song he so often
Scaled the ornaments of his lonely
Mantelpiece

Couldn't
Find
The
Coal
For the Fire
Edgar Allan Poe
Couldn't
Find
The
Coal
For the fire...

RACIAL PRIDE

The heat in the deep fires of our minds
Is getting dangerously hot
The longing to be more not less than mankind
Is to be satisfied with that which we've got.
The red angry blood of rage
Is seething inside
We are turning the page
For racial pride.

The white salesman now not so confident
Hide all they have to sell
Hiding behind their suitcase of resentment
Like hermits they returned to their shell
In astonishment our anger turns to rage
Bubbling and spitting inside
We are turning the page
For racial pride

So stamp your feet in white hysteria
Bang your fists on the table
For it is you who is and always was inferior
It is you who lies folorn and unstable
And in your historically immature temper you
will
(as you have in the past) unstable us culturally
But the problem lies in you still
Even is we leave your country

And in your historically immature temper you
will
(as you have in the past) unstable us culturally
But the problem is with you still
For you desperately seek your identity
Don't turn your tables on us

For we will return in rage
We boil and bubble inside
See as we turn the page
For racial pride.

The heat in the deep fires of our minds
Is getting dangerously hot.

YOUNG
WRITERS

MAXINE BENNETT

I have got six sisters and one brother. My mum is white and my dad Black British. My adopted parents are white. My hobbies are helping my mum look after the six children she minds. When I leave school I am hoping to be a car mechanic and have my own business. I am 14 years old.

BACK HOME

I'd go back home,
if I could.
To sea and sweet sunshine.
I'd sit beneath a mango tree
And smile boy smile.

But back home for me
is England
Where I was born and bred.
But just think if I wasn't born here,
Where I would be instead.

BASHSHAS MUBARIK

I am a seventeen years old Black British Pakistani. I have visited my Homeland a couple of times. Other than that I have lived all my life in Chadderton, Oldham. At present I am attending Grange Secondary School in the Sixth form.

BLACK HEART

Break my Black heart
Shake my glass heart
Yell so loud it shatters
Ain't that all that matters.

Rip my Black heart
Tear my silk heart
Claw it into tatters
Ain't that all that matters.

See my 'black' heart
See my 'bad' heart
It may rule my fate
But
it's never made me hate you.

GEORGINA PEMBERTON

*I have five brothers and sisters, they are
Black British. My parents come from St Kitts,
my Grandparents came from Nevis in St Kitts,
they are now dead.*

MINORITY AND MAJORITY

Play, work and rest everyday,
This is my life.
Learning and studying as hard as I can,
Trying to get qualifications.
But never will I get a job.
Just because my face is black.
Because I'm black.

I don't dislike white people
Yet white people dislike me.
White has money and power,
White is the majority.
And black.
We are the minority.

Don't give me sympathy.
I'm proud to be me
Young, Black and free
That's me.
Yes,
That's me.
Young, BLACK and free.

ANNE-MARIE THOMPSON

I was born in 1970 in Manchester, the youngest child of a Jamaican family. I am presently studying for 'A' levels in psychology and sociology, hopefully later doing a one year in classics. Most of my free time is spent thinking up plots for horror stories, reading books on parapsychology and occasionally writing the odd poem. My main ambition is to be the best horror writer of my generation; failing that, a good writer.

WHARA POSEUR

She sits there,
All smug. Grinning like
A banshee. Twittering
And wittering away.
Every few seconds
Out comes the mirror,
'Is me hair awright loves?'
'Can yer see a spot?'
'Don't yer think am beautiful?'
'Oh, 'eck look at me 'air!'
A luminous green comb
Is produced from nowhere.
War errupts between comb
And dry brittle hair.
A fit lad enters the classroom,
By the door.
The poseur's grin immediately
Widens, to show three broken
Teeth. To attract attention,
She laughs her hyena laugh.
A vomit coloured blouse
Is pulled from a bag and
Slipped over a head.
She struts around the
Class, on newly acquired
Six inch heels.
The fit lad is worried.
He thinks she fancies him.

**But the truth of the
Matter is.
She's after his mirrored specs!**

THINGS WERE HEADING THAT WAY!

A lifetime ago,
To catch up with.
Violent father,
Loving Mother.
And doing things for the best.
Sharon's secrets were no secrets.
I comforted,
Everyone comforted.
Everyone gossiped.

The boyfriends got older,
The love bites bigger.

Sharon left school,
15¾
College after sixteen weeks of freedom.

Before becoming,
Sweet sixteen,
She aborted a bundle of joy.

Hey Shaz remember me!
We had fun didn't we
Nine years of it, Remember...

Hey public, go away,
Shed some tears,
The rest is private O.K.

THE CONSTRUCTION OF TIME

Time shifts comfortably through time,
Neat,
Measured and accounted for,
Some,
Endless pain,
Endless joy,

Who will terminate time?

The seconds blend into minutes,
The minutes submit into hours.
The hours cling to make days,
The days grasp at the weeks.
The weeks stretch into years,
The years bask in the glory of decades.
The decades growing into centuries,
The centuries into new eras of time, place and
thought.

What is time?
Where does it come from?
Where does it go?
Why does it exist?
Who procureth it...?

MILKYWAY MOON

Milkway Moon,
Flying high,
Waiting to salute,
birds in blue sky.
Motioning clouds,
trying to keep,
Milkyway Moon,
from falling asleep.
Mountain peaks,
obscure the sun,
Milkyway Moon,
Let justice be done.
Milkway Moon,
Man in the Moon,
Guarding earth,
from disaster? Soon?
Milkyway Moon,
chocolate bar,
Nestle's white?
No, camouflage Star!

RELATIONS (PART 1)

They dribble in through the
front door. Inconspicuous
Relatives muttering nonsensical
greetings.
House tours are granted
And they stumble around,
Foolishly, praising everything.
Tea is offered, refused,
offered, accepted.
Biscuits? 'Do you think I
should George. Well go on
just this once.'
Soon Uncle Clyde donates a
joke. Polite laughter.
A hint of sarcasm? Perhaps.
Before they leave,
'you must come and see us
sometime. George was
saying only yesterday, we
don't see enough of you.'
'Of course, I'll come and see
you,' I lie through clenched teeth.

THE HILLS OF KEATH

An Awesome sight,
The hills of Keath.
Ten big men bold.

Most walkers look,
With open mouth,
and astonished eye.
They gasp,
then turn,
and flee.

THE ARGUMENT

He stands, swaying,
Like a drunken man.
She sits, book in lap,
Staring at him with
Wild defiant eyes.

They scream absurd
Obscenities at each other.
His drunken dance to the
Outsider is pathetic to see.
They are oblivious to all
Except their own anger.
Now and again there
Is a pause in the storm.
As they gather strength
For part 2 of the battle.

And now she stands
Arms flailing out
Striking air. Suddenly,
No warning. He
Swings around his
Arm, and deals her
A heavy blow to the
Head. She is momentarily
Stunned, before falling
Backwards. Onto the
Couch. She'll forgive
Him again. Tomorrow.

ASIAN LANGUAGE GLOSSARY

YOUR STORY SITA

Sita is the heroine of India's most famous epic; **The Ramayana.** An exemplary wife to Rama, Crown Prince of Ayodhya, she followed him into exile in a forest. The story of Rama and Sita is one of the great romances of world literature and the character of Sita has come down the centuries as a model for Indian womanhood. The abridged version of the story usually told to children, ends with Rama and Sita returning in triumph to Ayodhya to live and rule happily ever after following the defeat of Ravana, the demon king who had dared to abduct Sita from the forest. However, Valmiki's original epic in Sanskrit, has many dimensions and includes the episodes of the fire test and Sita's second exile which are referred to in this poem.

URDU

Accha	O.K.
Allah Pak	God, respect (Only Allah can do)
Baji	Big Sister
Burqa	Veil
Dupatta	Long scarf
Chana	Chick pea
Ghee	Fat for frying
Halwa	Semolina pudding
Hijab	A large veil which covers the head and body
Izzat	Personal honour
Jhumka	Dangling earrings of a classic style
Kameez	Long skirt
Kanteh	Earrings
Keema	Minced meat
Kothis	Villa or bungalow
Kurtha	Nightdress
Mithai	Sweetmeats
Muezzin	The Mullah who leads the prayer from the top of the mosque
Nikkah	Marriage ceremony
Panjangla	Jewellery covering the back of the hand and five fingers
Pillau	A savoury mixture of rice and vegetables, normally peas
Pourri	Fried wheaten pancake

Sari	Length of material normally 5 metres which is draped independently round the body, there are no stitches or fastenings
Sehr	Walks
Shalwar	Baggy pants
Sharm	Shame
Sharara	Baggy trousers fully pleated like a skirt, part of the marriage trousseau.

Kanta Walker

PATWA/PATOIS GLOSSARY

Patois has for many years suffered the indignity of being referred to as 'pigeon English'. In truth Patois is a language in itself, made up of a combination of Spanish, French, English, Portuguese and African languages. It was originally devised to resist the slave traders who attempted as far as possible to isolate slaves speaking a similar tongue in the hope that this would prevent them from rebelling and escaping. Human beings must communicate with each other: (remember that the slave traders considered all non-whites to be lower than animals) therefore Patwa stands as a language of struggle and survival.

Throughout the Caribbean there exists several different dialects. Trinidadian Patwa (a mixture of French/Spanish/English) is one form which is fairly accessible to speakers of standard English. The work of John Lyons therefore only needs to have certain terms explained.

Bobolee A stuffed effigy of Judas made on Good Friday morning and displayed all day, then beaten to shreds at evening time by the village youths.

Cascadura The Cascadura is a very bony,
(Cascadoora) thick scaled, freshwater fish.
(Cascadoux) Legend has it that anyone who eats this fish, no matter where

	in the world, that person must return to Trinidad to die.
Cheups	Pronounced — 'Steups' A noise made by sucking air through pursed lips and clenched teeth. An expression of annoyance. "To suck your teeth."
Fyzabad	The name of a southern town in Trinidad.
Mamaguy	To make fun of. To fool someone with smart talk or slick reasoning. To ridicule.
Pewah	A fruit 4cm/1½ inches in diameter, bearing in clusters. Bright red, fleshy, seeded, edible when boiled. A member of the palm family.
Pomme-arac (*Pommerac*)	A pear shaped fruit, red in colour with white cotton type flesh, containing a large seed.
Soucouyant	Pronounced 'soo-coo-yah'. A folklore character portrayed as an old hag, who transforms herself into a ball of fire at night and sucks the blood of her victims. She returns to her shed skin before daybreak. Legend has it that salt prevents re-entry and causes death.

JAMAICAN PATWA/PATOIS

Patrick Elly writes in his natural tongue of Jamaican Patwa which in its more conservative form differs more radically from standard English. For this reason the spellings below reflect the differences in grammar as well as punctuation.

an	and
aey	hey
badda	bother
becaw	because
bout	about
breddah	Brethren/Brother
caw	cause
cyaan	cannot
dat	that
dis	this
de	the
dem	them
dese	these
duh	do
fi	to
gat	get
galang	get along
gwaan	go on
homelan	homeland

I n I	This term is used by Rastafarians when talking about himself/herself, fellow Rastas and Haile Selassie, *He of all people.* It illustrates that no one person is independent of another but all members of one family I n I
inna	in/inner
livicated	A Rasta-style reinterpretation of 'dedicated', where the negative connotations of ded = dead are reversed by replacing it with the positive live = liv to get 'livicated'.
man	sometimes used to mean 'me'
mek	make
mi	me
mout	mouth
mus	must
neva	never
nu	know
nuh	no
outa	out of
pan	upon
sah	sir
seh	say
staat	start
suffah	suffer
sus	understand
tank	thank
tink	think
yout	youth

yu	you
wah	what
wen/weh	when
wrang	wrong
wudda	would have
wuk	work

Thanks to Judy Craven for her help and guidance in the preparation of this glossary and background of Patwa/Patois.

Further information available from Afro-Caribbean Language unit at the 8411 Centre, Moss Side Precinct, Manchester.
Tel 061 226 8411.

ABOUT COMMONWORD

Commonword is a non profit making community publishing co- operative producing books by writers in the North West and supporting and developing their work. In this way Commonword brings new writing to a wide audience.

Over a period of ten years Commonword has published poetry, short stories and other forms of creative writing. 'Black and Priceless' is the second title published under the 'Crocus' imprint. Forthcoming books include 'She says', a volume of women's poetry; and 'Now then' — a book of creative writing with a local history theme.

In general, Commonword seeks to encourage the creative writing and publishing of the diverse groups in society who have lacked or been excluded from the means of expression through the written word. Working class writers, black writers, women, and lesbians and gay men all too often fall into this category.

To give writers the opportunity to develop their work in an informal setting, Commonword offers a variety of writers' workshops, such as Womanswrite, the Monday Night Group, and Northern Gay writers.

Cultureword, which is a part of Commonword and which acts as a focus for Black writers, organises the Black Writers' Workshop. Cultureword also co-ordinates 'Moss Side Write' magazine, and a writing competition for Black Writers — the winners of that competition are published here. A full-time worker is promoting Black Women's writing.

In addition to writers' workshops and publishing, Commonword offers a manuscript reading service to give constructive criticism, and can give information and advice to writers about facilities in their immediate locality. 'Writers Reign' magazine contains both information and new writing.

Commonword is supported by North West Arts Association, the Association of Greater Manchester Authorities, the Commission for Racial Equality, and Manchester City Council.

The Commonword/Cultureword offices are at Cheetwood House, 21 Newton Street, Piccadilly, Manchester. Our phone number is (061) 236 2773. We would like to hear from you.

If you've enjoyed reading Black and Priceless, *why not try some of our other recent books?*

Holding Out: Short Stories by Women

Holding Out contains a compelling and challenging selection of writing. With both humour and pathos, this collection vividly portrays women's lives. The stories in the book take the reader from a still birth in 1930's Lancashire in 'The Confinement', through to a disturbing tale of child sex abuse in the Britain of the 1980s in 'Daddy's Toy'. 'A Pair of Jeans' describes how what may appear to be a simple item of clothing can wreak havoc in the life of an Asian family, whilst 'Nothing Happened' is an affectionately wry look at life on the dole. These are just a small selection from this collection of twenty-one stories, which demonstrates both the strength, and the variety, of contemporary women's writing.

"This impressive collection of new work is sincere and honest, and it's enjoyable because the women featured cope with their lives with strength, courage and most of all, humour."
(CITY LIFE 25/3/1988)
£3.50   156 pages   ISBN 0 946745 30 7

Poetic Licence

Poetic Licence is an exuberant and bubbling brew of poetry from a diversity of poets living and working in Greater Manchester. Their work celebrates the many pleasures of poetry — from the serious and intense, to the playful and humorous.

This book contains work from some exciting new poets. There's writing from the Black Writers'

Workshop, and Northern Gay Writers, as well as from 'Chances' — a group of disabled and able-bodied writers, and performance poetry from Stand and Deliver. Peter Street writes movingly of old age and disability, whilst Anne Paley looks at life in the '80s as a woman, there's poetry in patwa from Patrick Elly, and short witty pieces from Gary Boswell.

"There are many different emotions and moods to be found within these pages and, read in its entirety, the whole volume is disarmingly powerful ... Excellent value for money"
(CITY LIFE 20/11/1987).

£2.50   208 pages   ISBN 0 946745 40 4

Between Mondays
The Monday Night Group

This collection of poetry is the latest book from Commonword's Monday Night Group. It brings together some promising new writers with plenty to say about life in the city, sexuality, Catholicism and many other subjects.

'A Northerner's Nightmare' describes the horror of a Salford lad lost on the London tube; 'Asleep in The Afternoon' takes us back to schooldays; 'Sideshow Sexuality' compares an adolescent girl's experience with the life of the fairground. This is just a small selection from a wide ranging anthology, which stretches from ranting to romance, and from childhood to old age.

"By publishing this book, Commonword has encouraged writers who might not otherwise have put pen to paper, who have valuable lives to share with us"
(ARTFUL REPORTER Dec/Jan 1987/8).

£2.50   104 pages   ISBN 0 946745 35 8

Liberation Soldier
Joe Smythe

What should poetry address itself to in the 1980s? Joe Smythe gives his own answer in this collection of recent work. Using a variety of styles, he explores the discontents and disturbances of the times, from inner city riots to apartheid in South Africa.

Joe Smythe also takes a fresh approach to more traditional poetic themes, such as love, time passing and the appreciation of the natural world. Running through all his work, though, is a streak of satirical humour, which crackles away even through the most serious of these well-crafted poems.

"Joe is a poet ... with a cutting edge. He writes with a sting, sometimes with ironic humour about what he knows best — the effect on him of living in the '80s and the way he sees it affect others" (MANCHESTER EVENING NEWS).

£2.50   84 pages   ISBN 0 946745 25 0

Autobiography

Australian Journal: Alf Ironmonger   60p
In 1946, off the coast of South Australia, two young shipmates decide to jump ashore. This is their tale...
ISBN 0 946745 01 3   64 pages

Dobroyed: Leslie Wilson   £1.20
The unique inside story of one person's experience of a year spent in an approved school.
ISBN 0 950599 74 3   142 pages

Fiction

Nothing Bad Said £1.20
A collection of short stories by fourteen writers, dealing with issues and situations that affect all our lives.
ISBN 0 950997 6 X 96 pages

Marshall's Big Score: John Gowling £1.20
A book about a love affair, played out against the backdrop of the gay scene in London, Liverpool and Manchester.
ISBN 0 946745 03 X 76 pages

Turning Points: Northern Gay Writers £2.95
This collection of short stories and poetry explores moments of crisis — turning points — in the lives of a variety of characters, with various different conclusions...
ISBN 0 946745 20 X 120 pages

Poetry

Hermit Crab: Di Williams 30p
Using the imagery of the sea and the seashore, these poems tell of a daughter's journey towards independence.
ISBN 0 946745 15 3 28 pages

Consider Only This: Sarah Ward 30p
A selection of poems which captures the atmosphere of moorland, cotton mills and small town life.
ISBN 0 946745 04 8 28 pages

High Living: Ruth Allinson   30p
   In these poems, Ruth Allinson casts a critical eye
over social injustice and female exploitation.
ISBN O 946745 00 5   28 pages

Diary of Divorce: Wendy Whitfield   £1.00
   Wendy Whitfield reflects on the breakdown of
her marriage in a series of poems and cartoons.
ISBN 0 9505997 7 8   28 pages

Forthcoming Titles

She Says   £2.95
   Fact and fantasy combine in this compelling
selection of new poetry by women writers.
ISBN 0 946745 50 1 Publication date: 1st September
1988

Now Then   £2.50
   Memories of living and working in Greater Manchester, from after the Second World War up till
1980 — history with a difference!
ISBN 0 946745 55 2 Publication date: 3rd November
1988

Order Form

Title	Price	Quantity
Poetic Licence	£2.50	....
Between Mondays	£2.50	....
Liberation Soldier	£2.50	....
Australian Journal	£0.60	....
Dobroyed	£1.20	....
Nothing Bad Said	£1.20	....
Marshall's Big Score	£1.20	....
Turning Points	£2.95	....
Hermit Crab	£0.30	....
Consider Only This	£0.30	....
High Living	£0.30	....
Diary of a Divorce	£1.00	....
Holding Out	£3.50	....
She Says	£2.95	....
Now Then	£2.50	....

Please send a cheque or postal order (made payable to Commonword Ltd) covering the purchase price plus 25p per book postage and packing.

Name (block letters) _____

Address: _____

_____

_____ Postcode _____

Please return to: Commonword, Cheetwood House, 21 Newton Street, Manchester M1 1FZ.